MIRROR, SWORD AND JEWEL

The Geometry of Japanese Life

KURT SINGER

Edited with an Introduction by
Richard Storry

KODANSHA INTERNATIONAL LTD.
Tokyo, New York & San Francisco

First published by Croom Helm, London, 1973.

Published by Kodansha International Ltd., 12–21 Otowa 2-chome, Bunkyo-ku, Tokyo 112 and Kodansha International /USA., 10 East 53rd Street, New York, New York 10022 and 44 Montgomery Street, San Francisco, California 94104. Copyright © 1973 by the Kurt and Edith Singer Stiftung. All rights reserved. Printed in Japan.

LCC 80–84423
ISBN 0–87011–460–3
JBC 0097–789411–2361

First paperback edition, 1981

Contents

TO THE MEMORY
OF
KARL WOLFSKEHL

Introduction

BY RICHARD STORRY

It must be more than two years ago now since I received an unexpected letter from London, from Dr Eduard Rosenbaum, who got in touch with me at the suggestion of a mutual friend, Professor James Joll. Dr Rosenbaum informed me that he had the MS of an unpublished book on Japan, the work of a friend who had died some years earlier in Greece and who had lived in Japan during the 1930s. Would I be interested in reading it?

The package that arrived in Oxford a few days later contained just over 300 quarto pages of typescript. As soon as I settled down to read them I recognised that here was a work of audacious insight by an unusual man. Dr Kurt Singer, I discovered, had taught economics at Tokyo Imperial University and had then moved north to Sendai, to the Higher School in that city. He had arrived in Japan in the late spring of 1931 and departed, for Australia, in the summer of 1939. *Mirror, Sword and Jewel* was written after the end of the Pacific War, while the author was at the University of Sydney. It represented his considered reflections on Japan and the Japanese. It was clear that Kurt Singer brought to his study of Japanese characteristics a first-class intellect, nourished by a classical education and refined by more than twenty years of writing and teaching in Germany. His approach was metaphysical. Singer was an economist with the soul of a poet.

German–Jewish by birth and upbringing, he commanded an English style that only occasionally ignored the claims of euphony. This lent an added flavour to one's appreciation of the MS; but what imposed respect was the perceptiveness of his comments on Japanese attitudes and traditions. At times, it is true, he seemed to be writing about a society that had ceased to exist. But it was only in certain areas, and superficially, that his views could be described as dated. He had lived—as I had, when I first went to Japan—in an atmosphere infected by the poison of radical nationalism. But like myself he had been lucky enough to work in an academic environment, for the most part in a provincial city far from Tokyo. However, unlike myself, he was a mature scholar, with an established position in his own country, when he first set foot in Japan. Indeed, Kurt Singer's arrival in that country must have more or less coincided with his forty-fifth birthday. Of the 1880s, the decade in which he was born, Singer was to write:

> "The generation born at that great watershed had the advantage of growing up within a social framework which had not yet exhausted its last resources of coherence and stability. Their educators were eminently mature minds, their youth coincided with movements opening new horizons of thought and beauty, their wills were kept in tension by a growing but not yet critical antagonism of forces."[1]

It was perhaps, in part, this inheritance, confident and well-ordered, that enabled Singer to look beyond the ephemeral to the real springs of Japanese life.

His stature, mental and physical, was such as to make a most favourable impression on the Japanese. He was an authority on Plato—his work on "Plato the Founder" (*Platon der Gründer*) had been published in 1927—and he belonged to the circle of the imperious and visionary post-Symbolist poet, Stefan George. He was a friend and admirer of Maynard Keynes, who had started contributing articles soon after the First War to an economic journal edited by Singer in Hamburg. At Tokyo Imperial University he lectured on political economy and sociology. He was a versatile and productive writer for such recondite periodicals in Japan as *Shiso* ("Thought"). In short, he was everything that a Japanese would expect a European scholar to be. And he possessed a further asset. As a former Tokyo colleague recalls: "Dr Singer was an exceptionally small man for a European, smaller than myself, who am small even among the Japanese."[2] This, in Japan in those days, was a real advantage. He is still remembered to this day with great affection by his former Japanese students.

When he sailed from Europe Singer intended to spend no more than three years at most in Japan. He was technically on leave from the University of Hamburg. In the Preface to *Mirror, Sword and Jewel* he confesses "not to have felt bored during those eight years [in Japan] during a single quarter of an hour". And after he left the country he told an acquaintance that in Japan "there was always electricity in the air". But we may be sure that he would have resumed his career in Germany, had not Hamburg University deprived him of his Readership in the spring of 1933, on the grounds of his Jewish origin.

The persecution of the Jews did not leave German Jews in Japan unscathed. Tokyo Imperial University declined to renew Singer's appointment at the end of his three-year contract. However, the Higher School in Sendai (*Dai Ni Koto Gakko*) gave him a lectureship on a year-to-year basis. This too was terminated, in the spring of 1939, thanks to pressure on the *Mombusho* (Ministry of Education) applied by the Nazi Teachers' Association in Japan. As Singer was to remark in later years: "In Japan all foreigners are treated as unwanted as soon as they cease to be *persona grata* in their own country."[3] He must have been tempted to make much the same kind of comment about the country of his second exile, Australia.

It appears to have been on the advice of Keynes that Singer chose Sydney as his destination when he left Japan in August, 1939. But the first years, at least, in Australia were not happy. Singer's status as a Jewish refugee seems not to have been recognised. Indeed, from June 1940, until October 1941, he was interned as an enemy alien; and it was not until 1946 that he was able to achieve a certain security, thanks to an appointment in the economics faculty of Sydney University, after he had chosen to acquire British nationality.

Kurt Singer never married. At the outbreak of war in Europe in 1939 his only close relative was a younger sister in Hamburg.

In October 1941 she was sent to a camp in the East (Lietzmann-stadt) in which it is presumed she met her death.[4]

In 1957 some financial restitution was made to Singer by the Hamburg Senate. In his appeal to the authorities of that city and university he could speak with justice of "pressing sorrow, hindered endeavour and offended honour".[5] It was in the autumn of that year, 1957, that he returned to Europe, living for a time in Rome and Switzerland. Finally he settled in Athens, where he found a certain peace and happiness. In the words of one of his friends, "Greece gave him the fulfilment of an old longing (*Sehnsucht*)." He died there in his seventy-sixth year on 10th February, 1962.

In *Mirror, Sword and Jewel* Singer, reminding us that his chapters are based on observations made in pre-war days, declares (p. 60):

"I am still inclined to think that, in spite of legislative changes which may in the long run affect some social relations, the fundamental pattern that has grown through centuries, following its own organic logic, will not be readily changed in a political environment of great instability. If I should be mistaken Japan will have ceased to be the nation I have known, and my account will record a closed chapter of some memorable centuries of social history."

It must be said that many foreigners well acquainted with Japan, as impressed by the liberation achieved in the post-war years as they are depressed by the ugly competitiveness and materialism of the present day, believe that important areas of the Japanese tradition, in art, social life, and religion, have disappeared. The writer Mishima took his own life in 1970 precisely because he was convinced that Japan had ceased to be the nation he had once known. Mishima straddled the generation gap. It is not uncommon for younger Japanese, indifferent and sometimes hostile to their heritage, to be totally baffled by the *mores* of their elders. If Kurt Singer had visited post-war Japan how far, if at all, would he have revised his MS? It is perhaps vain to speculate. But it is worth noting that Singer's belief in the durability of "the fundamental pattern" is shared by such acute and experienced scholars as Chie Nakane and Fosco Maraini. The former argues that the basic nature and core of personal relations and group dynamics in Japan have scarcely been touched at all by the manifold changes that have occurred. Imported Western cultural elements, she tells us, "are always partial and segmentary". The "operating system"—the driving force—remains the same.

> "It is like a language with its basic indigenous structure or grammar which has accumulated a heavy overlay of borrowed vocabulary; while the outlook of Japanese society has suffered drastic changes over the past hundred years, the basic social grammar has hardly been affected. Here is an example of industrialization and the importation of western culture not effecting changes in the basic cultural structure."[6]

Dr Maraini turns the whole question inside out, as it were, with his *apercu*: "the Japanese have been modern since prehistory."[7] Indeed, central to Maraini's interpretation of Japan is his concept of *the future of the past;* from the earliest times to the present day there is "a pattern of continuity".

To my mind, at any rate, the passages in *Mirror, Sword and Jewel* that can be described as peculiarly redolent of pre-war Japan are not essential to Singer's main thesis, which is that "the Japanese mind and its products, at their best, bear the mark of two qualities rarely, if ever, united in one civilisation: nearness to origins (*Ursprunglichkeit*) and aristocratic distinction (*Vornehmheit*)" (p. 97). For example, recalling an everyday scene in pre-war Japan that is now much less common, at least in the big cities and towns, Singer refers to the gait of a Japanese woman carrying her child on her back—"she often pauses, seems to swing softly on the spot, casting a glance across the shoulder and humming an age-old song into the ears of the half-somnolent child"

(p. 35). This is a faithful evocation. The reader who knew Japan until very recent years will immediately acknowledge the truth of that description. It is now thought to be injurious to a woman's figure to carry the infant in the traditional pick-a-back. But the increasing use of baby-carriages does not mean a lessening of that devoted attention given, throughout its waking hours, to the Japanese child by the mother. The country remains a "children's paradise". The conscious and unconscious Japanese memory of childhood in Arcadia depends surely on the constant proximity, concern, and availability of the mother; if these are not removed, a pram is almost—if not quite—as satisfactory as a pair of shoulders.

Singer's reference to "nearness to origins" is related to his comprehension of the fidelity of Japanese instinctive feelings. He makes the impressive observation that the Japanese "are peculiarly sensitive to the smell of decay, however well screened . . . they resent haughtiness but adore unsullied greatness of mind and strength of will" (p. 39). It is a statement amply endorsed by a study of Japanese history, and by one's personal experience. Yet I know of no other foreign writer on Japan who has noted that point about the sensitivity to the smell of decay, *however well screened*. This is something which those who wish to understand Japan should never forget.

Indeed, Singer's reflections may serve as a practical guide. Of course he underlines traits and habits well attested by other witnesses. He points out, as others have pointed out, that in conversation and daily behaviour the main concern in Japan seems to be how to wrap up ideas, things, feelings; and he goes on to say that "wherever Japanese life is not governed by this law of laws behaviour is in constant danger of becoming arbitrary and uncouth, crude and repulsive" (p. 45). It is chapter 2 which discusses, in lively fashion, that "law of laws"—the phrase is, if one may use the term, a characteristic "Singerism"—and it deals with a perennial and significant aspect of Japanese conduct, still of fundamental importance although less prominent today than in the 1930s. But it is in a later chapter, *The Law of Harmonious Flow*, that the reader who is given a chance to visit or live in Japan, will find a piece of advice most helpful to his well-being.

"Let him, experimentally but unreservedly, behave according to Japanese custom, and he will instantly feel what a cell endowed with rudiments of human sensibility must be supposed to feel in a well-coordinated body. There is a bewildering number of conventions and taboos, in various degrees of unintelligibility; if these are mastered and observed, life becomes singularly easy and entrancing" (p. 64).

Singer suggests that the ultimate purpose of the Japanese system of ritual customs is "the transformation of everyday life into a quiet stream". This is what is meant by "Harmonious Flow". And it is undeniable that only by following Singer's advice will a *Gaijin* (foreigner) begin to savour the remarkable *cosiness* of Japanese domestic life. And if no effort at all is made to behave in Japan according to Japanese custom, the foreign resident, as Singer points out, "will remain a source of chronic wonder and anxiety to his environment". It was Lafcadio Hearn, entranced by his first years at Matsue, who used the imagery of a dream to describe the peculiar charm of the flow of ordinary social life in Japan. The foreign resident who fails to experience this phenomenon misses one of the best things that Japan has to offer.

Yet like Hearn, James Kirkup, and others who have wisely allowed themselves to be led far up the Japanese garden path, Singer comes to the end of the dream at last.

"Dark powers thinly veiled will not fail to do their saddening work, appearances and reality will diverge. But this awakening, recalling Prospero's *Epilogue*, does not detract from the magical charm of the dream as long as it was dreamt" (p. 67).

Related to "Harmonius Flow" is *The Law of Small Numbers*. Here Singer identifies a feature of Japanese life which has attracted a good deal of interest among sociologists and political scientists, both native and foreign. "The smooth flux of ordinary Japanese life" rests on a "dense tissue of small society relationships" (p. 82). And Singer makes the interesting and valid point that age groups and patron-client relationships may be at least as important as the family relationship. Indeed he suggests that excessive attention has been paid to the "family system", that this is in fact a late growth, transplanted from China, institutionalised by the Tokugawa Shogunate for political ends. The very rigidity of traditional family rules and rites, "contrasting sharply with the fluidity and suppleness peculiar to Japanese ways of life, points to a foreign origin and purposive exploitation" (p. 86). Here, however, Singer has in mind the enlarged family, with its "main house" and collateral junior branches. This phenomenon was characteristic of Japan when Singer lived there. It is by no means prevalent today.

But even by comparison with the small family, in which the natural ties of affection have always been strong, the age group and the patron-client relationship are of great significance. Anyone familiar with Japanese life will know how assiduously maintained are the friendships formed at school, in the same age group. As for the patron-client (*oyabun-kobun*) phenomenon, its importance can hardly be exaggerated. Singer sees a parallel between the Japanese patron-client relationship and the ancient Roman bond between a man of rank and influence and his many clients. To describe this relationship as "feudalistic"—a favourite term of the Japanese Left—is unhistorical; for the *oyabun-kobun* nexus is indeed much older; and it is to be observed, needless to say, in the most "progressive" circles of Japanese life.

Kurt Singer maintains that "it is one of the most characteristic traits of Japanese life that it has reduced the realm of genius to a bare minimum, with a rigour unknown in any other civilization" (p. 94). A little later he perpetuates an old fallacy, with his comment that the Japanese "invent few things", although they "excel in the art of adapting, adjusting, fitting" (p. 98). The process of assimilating foreign modes is compared with "the mimicry of animals, or the submission by women to a new fashion".

(Femininity is a Japanese trait to which Singer—rightly in my view—attaches much importance.) The truth, surely, is that, like any other people, the Japanese imitate foreign models for strictly pragmatic reasons. Up to a year or two ago it was common to read and hear criticisms of Japan on the grounds that the country had become fundamentally "Americanised". This ignored the staring fact that Great Britain, for example, has been increasingly "Americanised" during the last seventy, or even eighty, years. But the penetration of literary styles, governmental and business structures, journalism and the universities, sartorial fashions, and colloquial terminology, by trans-atlantic modes has by no means suppressed, although it may have marginally discouraged, the inventiveness of the British people. It is the same with Japan.

In two chapters concerned with Sino-Japanese "polarities", Singer exhibits a masterly command of the use of symbolism to drive home certain assertions on basic Chinese and Japanese instinctive beliefs and characteristics. They will probably irritate the scientifically fastidious as profoundly as they must enchant the mind that is drawn to metaphysical speculation. In these chapters Singer's insight into things Japanese is illuminating. He either throws a new light on a facet that is familiar, or brings out of darkness what seems to be a quite new feature of the scene.

"If there is a law governing this un-cosmic world of the Japanese, both in his highest modes of being where he aims at the Absolute and in his everyday life where he is concerned with mere utilities, it can only be a law of inescapable change and universal impermanence. In no literature of a great nation is there less room than here for the pure radiance of the stars and for the geometrical order of their courses; neither the Pythagorean harmony of the spheres nor the Platonic idea of ideas speaks to the Japanese. Identity, Measure, Immutability do not correspond to inborn needs of his soul . . . For everything leads the Japanese back to himself; to him seeing is a circuit. His is the existence of a Monad leading a

2

life that gravitates on an internal abyss of whirl-pool like forces" (p. 109).

Recalling that a monad is "an ultimate atom; an elementary organism", we see that the last line of that passage expresses Singer's concept of "nearness to origins" applied to the Japanese. The passage as a whole underlines the force of a later sentence:

"Metaphysics have never stirred the intellectual passion of the Japanese; who tend to take pragmatist attitudes and are always eager to shorten the circuit from one action to another" (p. 118).

For Singer exmphasises repeatedly the central importance in Japan of movement, of action, of inspired spontaneity. He contrasts this with the Chinese tradition of a symmetrical, balanced view of life and art. He refers to Japan as existing in "the realm of Time"; whereas China is in "the realm of Space". Space is linked with cosmic beliefs, order, and symmetry. Time is associated with *movement*. In Chinese writing, suggestive of perfect equipoise, the hand guides the brush in a plane perpendicular, at a right angle, to the paper. In Japanese writing the angle is usually oblique. In this difference Singer perceives an illustration of his theme. The departure from the vertical plane by the Japanese frees the impulse of movement "from the rigid pattern of symmetry and balance". And in every other sphere of Japanese art, according to Singer, "it is not space that rules . . . but time, duration, spontaneous change, continuity of movement" (p. 147).

An astute Korean soldier-politician once told me that Chinese and Japanese chopsticks symbolise the contrasting tempers of the two nations. The long chopsticks used in China are suited to a rounded, relaxed, personality, eating at ease, with little fear of interruption. The shorter Japanese *hashi*, on the other hand, are indicative of a people "on edge", eating in a hurry, alert against emergencies. Folklore of this kind—like nearly all "old wives' tales"—usually contains an element of truth. The tension, "the electricity in the air", ever present in Japan is certainly related to that impulse of movement in "the realm of Time" which Singer finds so significant.

Kurt Singer's last chapter, on the samurai, treats a fairly well-worn subject that seems, at first sight, to have not very much relevance to present-day Japan. Singer's examination is nevertheless instructive. In a revealing passage he observes:

> "Questions of honour are singularly ill-suited for statistical treatment. We have no means of knowing whether the majority of the samurai—or, for that matter any class in any country—did or did not remain below the standard set by codes and treatises" (p. 161).

I am sure he is right when he argues that samurai ethics imposed demands which were fully met only by a moral élite; that those who could not live up to such standards were, nevertheless, unable to deny their excellence. Thus, "it would be a serious mistake to believe that it was governmental propaganda that made the modern Japanese ready to fling their lives away and suffer what appears intolerable" (p. 166). Singer dismisses pre-war exploitation of the samurai image as vulgarisation, the work of propaganda in the service of acquisitive imperialist aims. It is extraordinarily difficult, it seems to me, to know what weight should be given to the factor of deliberate political manipulation of public opinion in Japan during the exceptional and critical years from 1931 to 1945. Singer clearly distinguishes between "the political and propaganda fictions" of the twentieth century and the process, in the Meiji era, of giving a new orientation to the concept of loyalty. For this concept, at the heart of the samurai code, was by no means necessarily associated with war or bloodshed. The most notable treatises on the samurai code in no way reflect a scale of values redolent of a military caste devoted to the arts of combat, and bent upon self-glorification. Yet Singer is bound to admit that the reader must face some difficulty in reconciling the ideal image with what "he has seen of, and read about, the callous insensitivity and unbridled violence of Japanese warriors".

The great merit of Singer's work is that it enhances our

imaginative understanding of traditional Japan. Even where well-informed critics might disagree with Singer, they must pay tribute to his lively, well-trained mind.

An English savant wrote of Stefan George:

"His circumstances favoured his adaptation of Greek ideas to his own life and prevented him from minding that the experience was fundamentally esoteric. He felt that if others could see things as he did, they would be the better for it. Nor did he think this impossible. Just as in the Middle Ages Germany had presented its ideal in such a masterpiece as the Rider of Bamberg, so George seems to have felt that it might again recognise such an ideal, and if it did, the gain would be great. The strength of his confidence and conviction shows how much George owed to his culture, how strongly it shaped his life. He had found his values in a study of the great civilisations of the past. It was only natural that he should interpret the present through what he had learned from them."[8]

Substitute Singer's name for that of George, and the words apply with precision to one who was, after all, a disciple of Stefan George. Indeed, they may serve as a memorial to Kurt Singer, and as an overture to his work.

I must acknowledge a debt of gratitude to Dr Eduard Rosenbaum for many things, above all for bringing Kurt Singer's study to my notice. I am indebted also to another friend of Singer's, namely Dr Georg Peter Landmann of Basel. I must express my appreciation, too, for much practical help, to Mr David Croom, Fräulein Marie-Louise Recker, Professor and Mrs Kan'ichi Fukuda, Dr Joshua Sherman and Miss Susan Kay.

RICHARD STORRY

St Antony's College,
Oxford.
June, 1972.

NOTES

1   K. Singer, "Keynes, A Memorial": *Kyklos*, Vol. V. Fasc. 1/2, p. 1. Berne; undated. [But Singer completed the article in 1950. R.S.]

2   Letter from Dr. H. Otsuka, Professor Emeritus, Tokyo University, May 1972. (To Professor K. Fukuda, Oxford.)

3   From an autobiographical statement in the possession of Dr Georg Peter Landmann, Basel.

4   *"Sie ist am 25 Oktober 1941 von Hamburg aus in den Osten (Lietzmannstadt) verschickt worden und ist nach menschlichen Ermessen dort vergast worden."* Autobiographical statement.

5   *ibid.*

6   Chie Nakane, *Japanese Society* (London, Weidenfeld and Nicolson, 1970), p. 149.

7   Fosco Maraini, *Japan: Patterns of Continuity* (Tokyo and Palo Alto, Kodansha International, 1971), p. 191.

8   C. M. Bowra, *The Heritage of Symbolism*, London, Macmillan, 1943, p. 125.

Preface

This book has been distilled from the experiences and meditations of a hundred months spent in Japan from May 1931 to August 1939, teaching and travelling, reading and musing, enjoying art and life, and harassed by increasing signs of an approaching catastrophe. There is but one way of knowing the mind of a foreign people from inside: to share its life, experimentally adopting its own style, allowing oneself to be swayed by its rhythm, both in the currents and seasons of daily intercourse and in the tides and revolutions of the spirit embodied and interpreted by its poets and painters, thinkers and founders of religion.

It was not only the curiosity of a student which lured me into this adventure. Since my boyhood I had been strangely attracted by the world pictured in the colour-prints of Harunobu and Kiyonaga, Utamaro and Hokusai, who made me wish to enter those frail and daring houses, to dwell near the infinitely graceful willows of their quiet rivers, to listen to the shrill punctuation of their music and to watch the flight of the wild geese across autumnal skies. The wish was granted when the Imperial University of Tokyo asked me to join its Department of Economics. I learnt to know in their own country the greater masters of art and literature, from Hitomaro to Basho, from the early sculptors to Sesshu and beyond, the weird beauty of the No-plays and the ascetic charm of the tea ceremony. These were not only aesthetic privileges. Whenever difficulties and tensions arose in everyday relations with Japanese friends and helpers, servants and officials, it often happened that better understanding was gained and equilibrium restored by reverting to the eleventh-century novel of Murasaki Shikibu, the fourteenth-century notebooks of Yoshida Kenko, to the seventeenth-century plays of Chikamatsu, and to the contemporary comedies of that astonishing actor-writer Goro. The first impulses and ultimate standards of a nation are best learnt at their pure sources. Much bewildering detail falls into its right place if seen from the centre and in the context of its formative epochs.

"You will find in Japan what I should like to call 'unity in disorder' in more than one sense", a Japanese diplomat said to me, smiling, the day before I left Europe, and I have often had occasion to appreciate the wisdom of this oracular formula. Seen from the metropolis, then darkened by the shadow of the great depression and by the brooding unrest which found its first alarming vent in the so-called Manchurian Incident a few months later, the country—torn between conflicting forces—resembled a vast untidy laboratory: disorder uniform, veiled by remnants of an old order neither alive nor dead, but preserving an uncanny degree of coherence and continuity. To discover the hidden laws of this life behind the apparently chaotic and often treacherously ambiguous aspects of the surface, was a delightful venture which kept my mind in constant tension. I confess not to have felt bored during those eight years during a single quarter of an hour. It is the harvest of those endeavours which has been for the most part gathered in these pages.

Reviewing the state of Asia at the beginning of the nineteenth century, Johannes von Mueller observed of the Japanese empire only these three words: "Japan remains locked." Since the great Swiss historian wrote there have been many changes in the fate and the relations of Japan, but his terse formula has only acquired a more disquieting significance. The Japanese islands have been opened to foreign intercourse; diplomatic nexus has been followed by mercantile exchange; students and travellers, experts and politicians, missionaries and writers have been sent out and welcomed; wars have broken out in which the remote island state suddenly rose to the status of a world power and with still greater suddenness fell into utter weakness and defeat. The state of virtual closure has, in a deeper sense, not ended.

Considering that this state of affairs is not only fraught with dangers in the sphere of international relations but presents the student of man with problems of some magnitude, the author of this book proposes to inquire whether the Japanese are in fact more enigmatic than the rest of mankind; what, according to the testimony of the past and present, are their persisting traits of character; what distinguishes the forms and standards of their social and political structure from our own; and whether this society has given birth and shelter to a culture different from that of other nations of the East and West.

A mirror, a sword and a jewel have been handed down from ruler to ruler in the Japanese dynasty as tokens of legitimate authority. Writers of the fifteenth century have interpreted them as symbolising the virtues the nation should cultivate: the mirror enabling us to see things as they are, good or bad, and thus becoming the true source of fairness and justice, the sword "firm, sharp and quickly decisive wherein lies the true origin of all wisdom", the jewel a moon-like symbol of gentleness and piety. It would be difficult to state more succinctly the standards of any inquiry into the mind of a foreign nation, and for this reason I have chosen them as the title of this book.

1

The Rhythm
of Childhood

I

Apollo's message: "Know thyself!" has never greeted a worshipper approaching a Japanese sanctuary. The mirror often seen at the entrance of a Shinto shrine does not invite the visitor to contemplate his image; its function, it seems, is to ward off evil spirits according to the ancient lore of Eastern magicians; it can be classed with the sacred rope (*shimenawa*) which demarcates a sacred precinct and assures its purity. It must not be confused with the mirror kept in many shrines as *shintai*, "god-body", seat of the spirit of Amaterasu-o-mikami or other deities.

"How should I be able to define the nature of the Japanese, being myself one of them?" replied a leading young Japanese mathematician, a mind of rare lucidity, when I had asked him to define the character of his nation. The Japanese excel in observing the flight of various birds, the sounds of different kinds of rain, the meaning of a certain slight twitching of the lips, a scarcely perceptible change in the direction of the gaze. To conceive, however, his own mind or soul as an articulated, structured unity is an idea altogether alien to him. Buddhist teaching has encouraged him to deny the existence of a soul, or self. States of mind, emotions, volitions are just occurrences, neither wholly objective nor subjective. Where his thought is directed towards an ego, individual or collective, his attitude tends not to be cognitive, but laudatory or deprecatory, the first as a rule in the case of the national self, the second in the case of

27

his own person. To "explain" means thus either to unmask or to extol, as became painfully clear in the never satisfied demand for the "clarification" of the national structure in the Minobe crisis of 1935.*

Japanese pronouncements on Japan before the resumption of contacts with the West in the nineteenth century were mostly mythological or eulogistic. Later writings echo in various modes merely the opinions of foreign observers and historians. Corresponding to the lack of original thought on their own national personality there appears to be a scarcity of penetrating ideas on the character of Western nations: these have been studied in much detail, but mainly with a view to finding solutions of problems facing their own nation. A writer, or a community, lacking true personality will not be able to see other persons or groups as structured wholes.

In the meantime Professor Watsuji's *Fudo* may well be taken to be the most significant analysis by a representative Japanese of the character of his nation and its main determinants.[1] His approach shows his scholarly acquaintance with Western methods, and a wide range of personal observation. Viewing man in his correlation with nature, as a child of the earth, rooted in a specific soil, he studies national character in relation to geography and climate, but he avoids that geopolitical fatalism which warlike governments find congenial to their policies. His attitude is that of a philosophical student of history who neither conceals the

---

* Minobe Tatsukichi (1873–1948), Professor Emeritus of Tokyo Imperial University and a member of the House of Peers in the Japanese Diet, was strongly attacked in the Diet and in the press by nationalists in 1935 on the grounds that his works on Japanese constitutional law, published more than twenty years earlier, were "disloyal". The unedifying campaign against Minobe was linked with strident demands for "the clarification of the national structure". This amounted to a witch-hunt against people in public life suspected of liberal and left-wing opinions. Minobe, an enlightened conservative, was obliged to resign his membership of the House of Peers and retire into private life. For some months he was given police protection. The personal sympathy of the Emperor and Premier Okada may have saved Minobe from prosecution but could not protect him from vilification by self-styled patriots. "The Minobe Affair" dominated much of the domestic political scene in 1935. [Ed.]

warmth of his patriotism nor allows himself to be carried away by quasi-myths and sentimental transports.

In order to acknowledge far-reaching affinities between landscape and civilisation one need not be a determinist of the naturalist school. The first systematic and most profound attempts to establish such correlations are due to Herder and Hegel, not to utilitarians and materialists. The Japanese mind seems by its very nature inclined to dwell in these border regions. No conception is more alien to the Japanese than the idea of a spirit, or mind (only the German *Geist* is adequate here), opposed to nature. In Japan man has never been torn from the familiar circle of animals, flowers and rocks; no divine will has given him command over his fellow-creatures; to him the very islands on which he dwells are elder children procreated by deities who are his own ancestors. Nor has Buddhist faith estranged him from living beings, whatever they may be. They too are capable of redemption; the same breath of the absolute, or nought, animates them and conveys enlightenment. The Japanese likes to tune his inner life to the rhythm of the seasons, submitting spontaneously and graciously to the powers of nature, unafraid of her abysmal dangers, feeling most free when yielding to her moods. Naturalism is here not a form of thought but a congenital disposition.

This nature, the geographical environment of Japan, is, according to Watsuji, first characterised by variety and contrast. Even if the extremes of the most northerly and southerly regions are left aside we find subarctic and subtropical features close to one another. Asiatic monsoons and Western-style cyclones are operating in the same season. Bamboo is often seen laden with snow. Wheat follows rice on the same field in the course of one year. The constant rhythm of summer and winter monsoons is broken by irregular storms. The differences of temperature are greater than in India, where high mountains shield the country from the cold winds of the Asiatic mainland. The popular calendar articulates the year into great regular segments after the pattern of the Chinese seasons with their majestic uniformity. In fact there is in Japan no calculable beginning of winter or summer, except for the custom-bound letter-writers of traditional greetings and warnings genially undisturbed by actual weather conditions. The monsoon-like summer rains may arrive sooner or later or fail to come. Spring and autumn change their climatic physiognomy almost every year. Real winter sets in when according to the calendar there ought to be a new spring; cold and snow often last into the days of the cherry blossom. Everywhere the capricious and incalculable appear to rule, aggravated by sudden excesses of floods and storms, earthquakes and tidal waves. It is as if nature had intended to teach man to be always on the alert and thus able to deal with catastrophe as a matter of routine.

Therefore the Japanese, according to Watsuji, has become "monsoon-minded", "cyclone-like", or "typhoon-like". He oscillates between extreme states, never resting in stable equilibrium, but opposing to violent and uncontrollable forces the virtues of silent suffering and stoic obedience. Food may grow luxuriously, and may perish overnight. Thus the Japanese is lured into passivity and encouraged to wait with patience; and while his sensibility is sharpened by external irregularities his feelings easily lose constancy. He is satisfied with short moments of fulfilment rapidly shattered as the cherry-blossoms most often are, and even his fighting spirit was often said not to be well sustained. Able to show great bravery, bordering sometimes on madness, he does not like to endure long hardship and adversity. Unlike the Russian, he prefers suicide to silent despair.

These observations tally well with Western judgments; and it is gratifying to see these confirmed by a student able to see things from within. What is more, such observations are corroborated by the highest authority of a nation—its poetry. The Japanese preference—except in their earliest and their latest epochs—for short poems of thirty-one (later of seventeen) syllables expresses the same character: a rhythm of high-strung emotions suddenly kindled and suddenly dying away, short phases of extreme tension surrounded by a sea of silence, a state of feeling crystallised in a single exclamation, cry, image, question; the few words hitting arrowlike their target with a clear poignant sound

not followed by reverberating echoes nor heralded by antici-
patory signs; never forming that wave-like, balancing, pattern
which is the soul of European and Chinese song and dance.

It has often been observed that Japan is a children's paradise.
A Japanese child, especially if it happens to be a boy—still more
so if it is a first-born son—is almost free from any restraint. The
child may do as it likes; it is very rarely scolded; if admonition is
administered it is done gently and without the parents showing
any anger; in the most severe cases the mother strikes his shin
with a rod: this is done only in the privacy of the home, however,
and without onlookers. Even on the street or in a railway com-
partment the child may shout, run or climb as its unruly heart
desires. Japanese children are spared the baneful "you must not"
to such a degree that they may be termed the real gods of the
country. They are the centre of the house and of the nation. Clad
in the brightest of colours they seem the only beings in Japan to
whom freedom of action and radiant looks are granted without
stint.

As the years grow in number a network of constraints begins
to be woven around these divine tyrants. As the child grows into
a youth and then into a young man, the demands of society
strengthen their hold on him, slowly and with increasing severity.
When the student graduates from his university he is like a tree
enclosed within a hard and colourless bark. A mask has been
growing on him, made out of discipline, tradition, self-restraint
and diffidence. Within this crust a thin sap of individual life is
still mounting and falling, but this flow too seems to be regulated
by the tides of the season and of the national destiny: the formation
of the mask is complete.

It is not fanciful to connect this unwritten law of Japanese
education with the emergence of those Japanese traits of character
which present the most striking contrast with Western styles of
life and thought.

In Europe the path of the individual seems to lead from the
swaddling stage to more and more unfettered wilfulness of
thought and action. The child is hedged in by numerous rules

and taboos; as he grows, new horizons of self-determination seem to open before him. The essence of academic life is in some Western countries termed academic freedom. The grown-up man or woman acknowledges, according to widespread political theories, only those forms of constraint which can be construed by them as conditions of more subtle forms of liberty. The eminently European idea of Hegel, who considered universal history as a continuous progress in the self-consciousness of freedom, may be taken as an expressive microcosmic projection of the life history of the typical Western individual. To the latter, time must appear as a one-dimensional movement towards the more desirable; and the concept of liberty implied in that process appears as a necessary condition of the mastery of increasingly complex tasks undertaken in progressive stages of responsibility. Liberty in its highest form receives the meaning of "freedom *for* . . ."; "freedom *from* . . ." being relegated to intermediate stages of the struggle towards perfection.

The contrast with the Japanese style of upbringing seems to be complete. To the Japanese complete enjoyment lies in an irrevocable past—an apparently utopian state, but one that has really existed, in which he had complete freedom to do as he liked, without incurring the dread sights and sounds of frowning faces or scolding voices. In that blissful state he was the centre of his universe, cherished beyond measure by the kindest and strongest beings he knew, his parents; whatever he did, prompted by desires springing up and vanishing in him like flowers and dragonflies, he felt their tenderness and joy in him undiminished. At the bottom of all his thoughts and longings and attitudes there will remain the memory of this golden age as a dreamy vision of what life can be, should be, will be—if only we should care to restore those pristine harmonies. Freedom will be associated here with anarchy, bliss with acting at the behest of the moment, authority with benign approval, the better future with a restoration of a past.

Isshin—renewal, renovation, calling back—is the Japanese form of revolution. Man is good, and no harm is done if he follows his unadulterated impulses; for it was thus that he gained and retained the love and admiration of his guardians. No later awareness of dubious inclinations and traits of his own nature, and of that of his fellow men, can destroy the vestiges of that primeval experience. Evil must be explained by pollution from outside, by malignant gods or spirits or dreadful substances; and their influence can be counteracted by lustration. The Japanese are shrewd and meticulous observers, nicely discriminating, capable of relentless sincerity whenever their instincts or instinct-like inclinations do not prevent their consciousness from coming into play. The strange disparity between the moral ideology of the Japanese and their actual lives thus suggests an explanation in terms of images drawing their strength from the ineradicable experiences of infancy. Only the unconscious is able to survive unquestioned and unquestionable in the presence of blatant contradictions in everyday observation.

Discipline, constraint, compulsion increase during the first twenty years of life in such a way that their growing severity is associated with increasing doses of enjoyment, self-assertion and social honour; they are correlated, therefore, with an increasing series of positive values. While his freedom of action is progressively diminished by inhibitions, rules, taboos, "oughts" and "ought nots", the boy, the youth, still more the young man, finds his sphere of knowledge, of will, of responsibility, of fancy, more and more extended: there is loss balanced by gain, and probably overbalanced. Tightening discipline is easily, and with growing insight, perceived to be the price paid for the desirable advantages of adult existence. The Western "freedom for . . ." finds its equivalent in the "constraint for . . .". Here again the strange readiness of the Japanese to accept the yoke of conventions, constraints, inhibitions, which to the Westerner would appear intolerable, seems to be rooted in unconscious layers of individual experience for which there are few analogies in Western society; except in the price exacted by the severe rules of old aristocratic circles, and in the self-imposed limitations within which the writer of a sonnet or composer of a fugue had to work.

To correlate the imposition of social discipline with the granting of increasing rights to the individual is not a technique invented by the Japanese. But it is a peculiar trait of the Japanese way of upbringing that with them discipline and constraint, at least during their decisive stages, are imposed less from outside, by men of greater age and terrifying authority, than by members of the same age group. In a Middle School, and still more in a Higher School, it is the pupils of the same form who tighten the network of "ought" and "ought not", according to their sentiment, belief, or waywardness. The pressure exercised by a "common will" on each pupil is not resented as an intrusion by the group into the life of the individual; for the group is conceived of as the individual's better self. More correctly, he does not live outside his group, with which he has come to feel identified, and to whose decisions and movements he contributes in such a way that he can scarcely distinguish his own contribution from that of his fellows. In the latest stages of Japanese education, when the university student becomes free of personal ties except those binding him to his family and school-group (which survives throughout his life), it is a more diffuse, but not less severe, pressure that makes him move in a tightening set of restrictive rules—namely the intangible spirit of the country, *yamato damashii*, or *kokutai*.*

But here too he is not confronted with a force supposed to exist outside his own self. What confronts him is the spirit of his ancestors, of the heroes of his country, of the very soul of the islands, trees, rocks and sanctuaries. And this lives on in the unwritten laws which in so many respects resemble the "paternal customs" of ancient Greece. Paradoxically enough, a process of education ostensibly preoccupied with the development of the rational abilities of the individual culminates in his growing up

* Singer's comments here are no longer topical. Pre-war patriotism has not been resurrected; and such amuletic terms as *Yamato Damashii* are still (1972) unfashionable. *Yamato*, strictly speaking the historical name of a province south of Kyoto, has been used traditionally as a name for Japan. *Yamato Damashii* = "the Japanese spirit". *Kokutai* = "national structure". Both terms acquired strong emotional significance in pre-war days. [Ed.]

to become a member of a mythical body to which he sacrifices his life and thought in order to receive his true self. Wherever this process is disturbed an anarchical state of mind is sure to develop, according to the same law that makes nihilism the end result of European attempts to replace reasonable freedom—as the goal of education—by a cult of the irrational.

II

The Japanese claim to be closer to nature than the people of the West (paradoxical to those who have observed how much convention, artificiality, and selectiveness enter into the Japanese cult of nature) seems to be rooted in dim recollections of childhood experience, and to be patterned after them. Nature conceived of as a soothing, nourishing, refreshing source of life, immeasurably benevolent, is a projection of the mother not separated from her children by a painful process of weaning.

For years the child is carried on the back of the mother, strapped or carried in a pouch-like fold of her padded over-garment, sharing in a half-drowsy state her warmth and her rhythm, robbed of free movement of his limbs but feeling sheltered and close to the maternal body which to him means life, protection, company and goodness. The unconditional surrender of the adult Japanese to the rhythm of fate, his apparently voluptuous contentment in being buffeted by the great forces beyond his control, his horror of isolation and his satisfaction in yielding to circumstances appear to be moulded on the traces left in his unconsciousness by those securely fettered and lovingly balanced states of early childhood. Can it be that the mechanically rolling motion of the pram, experienced in infancy, has prepared the Westerner to accept quasi-automatic progress in a given direction as the most natural form of change? The gait of a Japanese woman carrying her child on the back is not suggestive of such linear transport: she often pauses, seems to swing softly on the spot, casting a glance across the shoulder and humming an age-old song into the ears of the half-somnolent child. To return to that semi-conscious state, when one was carried to and fro by a power larger than oneself, appears to remain, even in adult life, the chief aim of internal discipline and external accommodation.

Father is a more remote, august, figure. He is not called upon as a last reserve of sternness and punitive power. If bodily chastisement is resorted to, it is usually administered by the mother, who in Japan, as in all oriental and classical countries, is and remains the "mistress of the interior", wielding unquestioned authority within the four walls. It is outside the gate that the dominion of the male begins and ends. To his children he is in some degree god-like; strong, helpful, loving, and removed from petty affairs. As long as he is in the house neither his time nor his nerves are spared. Tired or not, he will coach the boys and make toys for all. It is difficult to say whether the children take more pride in him or he in them.

In the West we have learned to trace the origin of many conflicts and neurotic disturbances of later life to infantile experiences and tensions arising out of the triangular relations of father, mother, and child; the mother standing between father and child, or the father appearing as an intruder in the mother–child relationship. The old style of Japanese family life seems to reduce the occasions for the emergence of such conflicts. The rules of customary behaviour imposed on the Japanese man go very far in preventing the child's trust in its absolute hold on its mother from being threatened by the exercise of marital rights. The child's feeling that his mother belongs to him, more than anyone else, is never disturbed. The long nursing period, with the unlimited demands it can make on the mother's milk, and the experience of being carried in close proximity to the mother's body are the basis of this feeling. Confucian rules which limit marital intercourse to a formalism, leaving no room for visible and audible raptures, suppress everything that could evoke the slightest traces of premature sexuality even if the child is sleeping in the parents' bedroom or in close proximity to it. The husband has to seek more Dionysiac exuberance in other quarters; the wife seems to find her most intense gratification in nursing her children.

It is probable that paternal authority is the product of a long and tenacious struggle in which father-right slowly vanquished mother-right. Some episodes of early Japanese history recall a period when the outcome of the struggle was still undecided. In the third century A.D., for example, it was the right of the mother to give a name to her child; and the strict subordination of women was not known before the age of late feudalism. Traces of matriarchal customs can be discovered today in remoter parts of the country.

Paradoxically enough in a race of warrior traditions and obviously virile virtues, the male Japanese can surprise us by distinctly feminine traits. It was an American astronomer, Percival Lowell, who first drew attention to this fact. He sees feminine traits in the delicacy, daintiness and love of dignity displayed by the Japanese, as opposed to the coarseness, directness and originality which (according to Lowell) characterise male-minded nations.[2] It is woman who by her comparative weakness is induced to subsist by adaptive change. Following the ways of the chameleon, she dissolves into her environment; while the male preserves his finite cast. The Japanese resemble the tribe of those who conquer by yielding. Their faculty for adaptation borders on a readiness to be hypnotised. First the civilisation of China and, later, Western ways of life exerted such a spell that for some time the Japanese seemed to have lost the consciousness of their own identity in a quasi-somnambulist urge to do what was suggested by the magic wand.

The sword in one's hand, the spear, even the word uttered, may gain such a hypnotic power that the idea of personal responsibility appears alien and remote. Camouflage here is not a technique, but an organic function. To say only what the interlocutor thinks or would like to think is, to the Japanese, not only a rule of etiquette but also an instinctive urge. It is his way of unconsciously responding to a given situation, irrespective of the bifurcation of truth or untruth. The process that creates a Japanese poem or painting does not resemble the sculptor's act of giving shape, form, definition, freeing a virtual beauty from the casual contests of matter and mind; it finds its nearest analogy in the sighing of a woman, the formation of a smile, the playful but irresistible gesture of her hand as it evokes a memory or rearranges her hair. The greatest even among the prose writers of Japan have been women, from Sei Shonagon and Murasaki Shikibu to Higuchi Ichiyo, and all of them are more feminine than the greatest of European poetesses, not only in their sensibility but also, and above all, in their style.*

The strong presence of female traits in the psyche of the Japanese will appear less strange if it is recalled that the most virile warriors of antiquity, the Spartans and the Romans, preserved traces of mother-right longer than the Athenians or the Teutons. Again, the hard-fighting Arabs of the desert, as Charles Doughty noted, were in aspect and behaviour more than half feminine.[3]

It is obvious how well upbringing in Japan is adapted to the production of female characteristics in male children. The long and flawless intimacy uniting child and mother throughout the first formative years must lead the child to identify itself with the mother by an unconscious process stronger and more far-reaching than the conscious emulation of the father, however greatly he is esteemed. Japanese boys in their earliest years seem even more shy than girls. The rudest and most violent Japanese god, Susanowo-no-mikoto, wails when his father entrusts him with command over the sea: he desires nothing else but to go to the netherworld in which his deceased mother dwells. The readiness of the Japanese to die, casting away their lives or dying by their own hands, may echo this desire of their divine ancestor.

The gladness with which the Japanese surrender their wills, granting to "circumstances" an authority that seems scarcely resented, their contentment in feeling the pulse of events regu-

* Sei Shonagon (*c.* 968–*c.* 1025) was a lady-in-waiting at the imperial court in Kyoto; famous for her collection of essays, *Makura no Soshi* ("Pillow Book"). Murasaki Shikibu (978–1015?), also a court lady, is renowned for her romantic novel, *Genji Monogatari* ("The Tale of Genji"). Higuchi Ichiyo (1872–1896), a genius whose short life was a constant struggle against poverty, won lasting acclaim for her works, especially *Takekurabe* ("Comparing Heights"). [Ed.]

lating their existence even if it shatters their dreams and frustrates their endeavours: all these signs of passionate passivity in an eager, ambitious, people must have been nourished, confirmed, and reinforced by those mother-child relations that shape the warp of the psyche's fabric. In China male-minded Confucius, state-bound, stern, with an unerring sense of the definite, stands at the side of Laotse, the worshipper of the dark female, of water seeking the lowest level, of not-doing, of the void and the weak. In Japan the female spirit seems to be harnessed to the chariot of the patriarchal State but remains its secret aim and ultimate measure. Seeing a Japanese mother in the street, serenely sauntering and humming, with her child attached to her back, one feels that it is through her that the stream of Japanese life runs and refreshes itself. The over-busy and excessively self-conscious males appear, compared with her, a mere protuberance, unattractive and lacking authenticity; useful or noisesome instruments, hardly initiated into the mystery of being.

III

The Japanese will accept domination, but only by men devoid of moral flabbiness, cheap sentimentalism, and corruption hidden behind a mask of sternness. They are peculiarly sensitive to the smell of decay, however well screened; and they will strike at an enemy whose core appears to betray a lack of firmness. They resent haughtiness but adore unsullied greatness of mind and strength of will. It was not only Perry's "black ships" that brought about the reversal of the Japanese attitude towards the Western powers in the years preceding the Meiji era: of not less importance was the dignified and intrepid behaviour of the first envoys, who dared to look into the Dragon-face of the Shogun, hitherto believed to bring death to the beholder.

The Japanese attitude to her enemies—China, Russia and others —has often been tinged with a feeling of contempt springing from an intuitive sense of manifest or threatened decay, loss of manliness, relaxation of moral fibre, behind imposing façades. Japan seeks the friendship and guidance of a foreign power so long as that nation is strong, certain of her will and mission and able to command the ready sacrifice of individual happiness for the common good. Japan swings with astonishing promptness from enmity and self-assertion to friendship, conciliation, submissiveness, whenever she bites on granite. The transition from xenophobia to collaboration was equally remarkable after Japan's defeat by the T'ang armies and fleets in the seventh century, following the dispute over Korea, and after the crushing demonstrations of superior power against Satsuma and Choshu in the middle of the nineteenth century. Conversely, as soon as the Japanese sensed the impending decay of the T'ang Empire in the ninth century diplomatic intercourse was broken off.

The attack on Germany's Eastern possessions at a time when she seemed at the zenith of her power, and in spite of the distinctly pro-German sentiments of the Japanese army, may be ascribed not only to a realistic calculation of naval capabilities, but also to an instinctive assessment of the internal weakness of the Kaiser's Reich.*

In this as in other fields the Japanese seem to have retained an animal-like, quasi-instinctive, knowledge of the weakness and the strength of actual and virtual adversaries—without, it is true, the unfailing precision of such zoological judgment. Their readiness, in the face of apparent odds, to attack wherever they believe they can smell decomposition makes them appear as true successors of the Huns, Avars, Mongols, and other "scourges of God".

Wherever there is contempt normal behaviour no longer exists. When wars were fought by knights or samurai who respected each other as embodiments of the same spirit and valour, deeds of cruelty were rare. It was not possible to see in another knight the impersonation of the devil, a being of inferior constitution, or the victim of eternal perdition. Religious or racial wars are of another kind; they tend to extinguish the male popu-

---

* The reference here is to Japan's participation in the First World War, when Japanese forces occupied the German islands in the Pacific and besieged the German-leased port of Tsingtao in Shantung. [Ed.]

lation, or at least to terrorise it into subjection by every method available. In the footsteps of such wars are apt to follow those internal wars usually termed revolutions. That Nazi Germany, which adopted Bolshevist terror methods in fighting internal and external enemies, was the teacher of Japanese army leaders would go far to explain why Japanese soldiers could be accused of having committed inhuman deeds on a scale unknown in former Japanese warfare. What was at work here was not only a propensity to emulate what appeared as the latest manifestation of the spirit of the age; the Second World War assumed, in more than one aspect, the character of a revolution (and counter-revolution) and followed in many ways the pattern of such conflicts.

IV

Generally speaking, the Japanese seem to prefer cutting and stabbing to shooting; the cult of the sword, the sport of *kendo* (fighting with bamboo swords), and a general liking for archaic weapons, seem to point in this direction. Hand-to-hand fighting has usually been esteemed more highly than the art of hitting from afar. Such has been the attitude of every aristocratically-minded warrior class. Military experts have noticed that as late as the nineteen-twenties there was a marked reluctance on the part of the Japanese to avail themselves of the latest mechanical improvements. This tendency appears to have been overcome so far as the army leaders were concerned, but it may have subsisted in the men and among junior officers. In every type of man in whom the primitive "killer" is waiting there must be a preference for methods of fighting that allow him to see and feel the enemy dying under his hands. The Japanese tactics of ramming planes and of crashing into ships must be explained not only by the ideology of self-sacrifice but also by the satisfaction these methods seem to give: the Japanese appears to enjoy the deadly bodily impact, even at the expense of his own life.

In the practice of *kendo* another trait of primitive psychology can be discovered: the unwillingness to stop if the adversary has received a mortal blow. The successful attacker continues to hit and hack, as if unable to control the movements of his weapon. This trait is confirmed by the tradition that a Japanese sword will go on killing and killing if it has once been drawn from its sheath. *Kendo* duels, which begin within the strict forms of medieval chivalry, seem to end (to a foreign onlooker) in a mutual cudgelling. In a famous *Kabuki* play, dealing with the life of Akechi Mitsuhide, the hero is shown as if drawn forward by the demonic forces propelling his spear towards the next room, where instead of the enemy he pierces, after ramming the door, his own mother.* It is as if the Japanese were still investing their weapons with that magical power which early man must have experienced when they felt the first weapons of stone and metal emerge in their hands.

"In Malabar", we read in Pinkerton's *Voyages and Travels*, "was a custom by which the Zamorin, or king, of Calicut had to cut his throat in public when he had reigned twelve years. In the seventeenth century a variation of his fate was made. He had to take his seat, after a great feast lasting twelve days, at a national assembly, surrounded by his armed suite, and it was lawful for anyone to attack him, and if he succeeded in killing him, the murderer himself became Zamorin."

It is interesting to note that in *sumo* wrestling among Japanese boys the scene often resembles that of the Malabar zamorin fight. A boy is attacked by a number of opponents, each of whom he has to fight one after the other, picking them in the order he thinks profitable. Thus a Japanese is accustomed from boyhood not to be dismayed by a fight against superior numbers; and he is taught to use as his strongest weapon the fear he can inspire by looks, shouts, movements. It is astonishing how completely mild-

---

* Akechi Mitsuhide (1528–1582), a warrior lord, turned against his suzerain, Oda Nobunaga, the most powerful man in the country, and killed him, thereby acquiring a supreme position, which endured, however, for only a very brief period. Akechi Mitsuhide was defeated, and Oda Nobunaga's death avenged, by Hideyoshi. Indeed his ascendancy lasted for barely a fortnight: hence the old saying, "*Akechi no tenka, mikka*" (Akechi's power lasted only three days). [Ed.]

mannered, sensitive, literature-loving boys are transformed into ferocious-looking, madly-fighting creatures of the jungle—just for the duration of the fight. One moment later they bow to each other politely, thank their adversary, and continue to think of Shelley, or Basho, Kant or the Lotus Sutra.

The sudden change from the refined representative of a subtle civilisation into the instinct-bound man of the Stone Age, and back again to the first stage, can be observed on the sports-ground of every school. Japanese custom and law have strictly barred outbreaks of those primitive fighting attitudes from the internal sphere of national life, while carefully keeping them intact for national emergencies. The contrasts present in every man are here allowed to grow to greater extremes than in our own civilisation, which, however sadly distant from its Greek source, still cherishes some remnants of measure and proportion.

NOTES

1 Dr Leopold Scheidl, *Betrachtungen über das Buch von Professor Tetsuro Watsuji, Fudo, Ningengakuteki Kosatsu.* (Views on the book, "A Climate; an Anthropological Interpretation" by Professor Tetsuro Watsuji, Tokyo, 1937.)

There is a translation of *Fudo* by Geoffrey Bownas: *A Climate, A Philosophical Study*, Tokyo, 1961. [Ed.]

2 Percival Lowell, *Occult Japan, or the Way of the Gods, an esoteric study of Japanese personality and possession*, Boston, 1894, p. 283 *et seq.*

3 Charles Doughty, *Arabia Deserta*, London, 1921, Vol. 1, pp. 238, 266.

2

The Mists
of Concealment

No people could be less entitled to complain of being misunderstood, unknown, or neglected than the Japanese, whose first and last urge is to lead a life unseen by others. "Every Englishman is an island", observed the German poet-philosopher Novalis, at the end of the eighteenth century. Equally, the Japanese can be called "a walled island hidden by clouds". This is more than a simile expressing the reactions of a foreign spectator. The first Japanese poem (attributed by the *Kojiki* to the god, Susanowo-no-mikoto*) evokes and praises such a cloud-enclosure:

> "Eight clouds arise.
>   For the spouse to retire (within)
>   The eight-fold fence of Izumo
>   Make an eight-fold fence.
>   Oh! that eight-fold fence."

The sacred mountain, Fuji-san, enveloped by clouds and almost disappearing in them, is felt by the Japanese to be more beautiful than when the unbroken outline of its majestic form is clearly

* The *Kojiki* is the first Japanese history, compiled early in the eighth century A.D. from the recollections of a master narrator of ancient traditions (a woman of 65, Hieda no Are). The work consists of three volumes, replete with mythology. In this mythology Susanowo-no-mikoto is the storm deity, and he is represented as a most violent destroyer, at odds with his sister, Amaterasu-o-mikami, the sun goddess. [Ed.]

revealed. Japanese writings, prose as well as poetry, suggest rather than express, satisfied with hints and intimations, shunning exposure. Traditional Japanese singing demands the repression of the voice, displaying strength of emotion by muffling it, never allowing it to flower bird-like into free flows of expression. Most of all this is true of the *utai*, the sung parts of the *No* plays, mystery plays which culminate in the dance of a mask and in the vanishing of the god it represents. They have a special word (*kamigakure*) for this sudden withdrawal of divine appearance.

In every gesture of daily life, in the style of conversation, in the proper form of giving a present, the main concern, it seems, is how to wrap up things, ideas, feelings. Wherever Japanese life is not governed by this law of laws behaviour is in constant danger of becoming arbitrary and uncouth, crude and repulsive. It is as if the Japanese, not content with living in a mountainous archipelago all too often visited by mists and clouds and rainstorms, had attempted, from the very beginnings of their civilisation, to reproduce in their social and cultural life an intensified image of their natural surroundings—an interior scenery veiled in vapour, divided into small compartments by mountain ranges, bays, and seas. Wherever they go they make a network of walls and fences behind which to retire: unwritten rules, ceremonies and taboos.

To the casual observer, Japanese domestic life, in its waking and sleeping hours alike, seems strangely devoid of privacy. The ordinary Japanese house affords little freedom from prying looks and unsolicited participation in practically all details of household routine, especially in the summer, when the "walls" become little more than a system of slender poles and frames, marking off, rather than shutting off, the interior of the house from its surroundings. The communal style of public baths seems carried to extremes incredible to the Western traveller. Intimate details of personal life are freely asked and talked about. No limits of any kind appear to inhibit the reporter's curiosity and the policeman's zeal.

What fails to be observed by most foreign visitors is the unseen screen behind which the Japanese withdraws whenever he chooses, skilfully parrying all those inquisitive looks and awkward questions which catch the foreigner defenceless. The Japanese knows how to draw around himself a wall of inscrutability and silence which allows him to live the life he likes best, shy, reserved, self-centred. The Japanese language is admirably equipped for such a style of life. Rich in ambiguities, elusive terms, indefinite constructions, it is a tool more for withholding and eluding than for expressing and stating. These tendencies are inherent in vocabulary and syntax; they are reinforced by the fact that the spoken word is often not understood until its Chinese ideogram is known, while this ideogram can often not be pronounced correctly upon mere reading. Nobody deplores the resulting measure of haziness. It is by higher degrees of clarity and precision that the Japanese would feel inconvenienced.

It would be rash indeed to ascribe purposeful intent to such behaviour. In many cases it will in fact serve to withhold from the outer world the knowledge of devious ways, or the expression of an uneasy conscience; it may help to gain advantage by profiting from darkness, or by making other people feel uneasy. In most cases, however, nothing is gained, in a pragmatic way. Nevertheless, the will to disappear behind a wall assumes the force and urgency of an instinctive reaction or a powerful passion. Is it a legacy of past centuries when governmental spying was universal and all-pervasive? Is it a natural reaction within Eastern nations, bound in every detail of everyday life by communal ties so strong that within the individual there emerges an instinct for seclusion, in order to counterbalance the immoderate demands of the group to which he belongs? Are these nations (for what we note in the Japanese is largely valid also for the Chinese and other Asian races) nearer to the wisdom of nature, which envelopes every living being with a protective sphere of darkness? No life can grow in the full glare of unmitigated light and unceasing discussion—a lesson the progressive Western world has still to learn, or re-learn.

Whatever the cause of this will to disappear behind a screen of wood, of words, or of customary behaviour, the real difficulty of understanding a Japanese begins only after these defence works of the individual have been penetrated, a process requiring more time and tact than the foreigner is apt to anticipate. To be admitted to the intimacy of a Japanese home is difficult and rare, for it means admittance to the presence of the ancestor-gods that live on the god-shelf of the main room. To master the complex framework of ceremonial is only slightly less difficult. For there will be no whole-hearted teachers. Books are of no avail except for giving historical reasons for "what is done", reasons generally unknown to the contemporary Japanese. But even if all these difficulties have been overcome, the foreigner well versed in Eastern lore and custom will often be at a loss to find the real motive prompting the behaviour of his Japanese friends, or to foretell their future attitudes. It is from such experiences that the idea of the perturbing inscrutability of the Japanese has grown; and the Westerner expects behind the impassive face of his acquaintances the presence of a dreadful or alluring secret. But in truth, here as in the story of the veiled image of Sais, there is nothing behind the veil. The Japanese are difficult to understand, not because they are complicated or strange but because they are so simple.

By simplicity I do not mean the absence of a multiplicity of elements. Few Japanese, except those who dwell in the remote villages, are "monoliths" and of archaic simple-mindedness. The language and literature of the Japanese are extremely rich in emotional shadings and in synonyms conveying subtle differences of meaning. The religious practice even of the ordinary man is highly complicated: he is liable to be Shintoist as a Japanese, Buddhist in face of death and suffering, Confucianist as a social being in general, personally often a Christian, and, as a man of science, a materialist. Behind the placid façade of correct demeanour he is apt to harbour a fleeting crowd of heterodoxies, doubts, sudden adventures, and variegated pastimes. Whatever he may be, he never resembles those schematic scarecrows figuring in text-books as first approximations to the image of man.

The cause of what strikes us as alien and impenetrable in Japanese minds is not the presence of a bewildering array of conflicting elements in their psyche, but rather the fact that no conflict is felt to exist between them. For they appear to us as clearly antagonistic. We are familiar enough, from our own experience, with the phenomenon of people living on different intellectual or religious planes, with their private and public lives not well-matched, or with their aesthetic tastes, their erotic leanings and their moral standards sadly at odds. However, in a predicament of this kind the typical Westerner feels himself to be the victim of conflicting duties, ideas, or cosmic forces. He will try to reconcile their claims or admit tragic defeat. Not so the Japanese: for him there is no urge here to struggle or to despair. Conflicting powers are reduced to ceremonial forms allocated to well-defined places and times and occasions: Buddhist for funerals, Shintoist for marriage rites, Christian for abstention from drinking and smoking, materialist for scientific working hypotheses. Conflicts are not fought out. They are eschewed. A solution forcing recalcitrant elements into a higher synthesis is not even aspired to. On the highest plane of Buddhist meditation all opposites are wiped out as irrelevant or phantasmal. The goal is to reach a state of mind in which the demarcation line between mind and matter, subject and object, man and universe, all and nought, has ceased to exist. In everyday existence the struggle for synthesis is replaced by an uncanny ability to fling oneself swiftly from one plane or branch to another.

It is not only in the spheres of thought and religion that these phenomena can be observed. It is still more puzzling to find that members of one of the most refined aesthetic civilisations exhibit bland indifference to the ugliest minglings of incompatible forms. No Japanese seems to realise that a hat cannot be put on by a person in *kimono* and *haori* without producing aesthetic disharmony. Nobody appears to be aware of the fact that the upper edge of a Western singlet (which is not meant to be seen at all) must destroy the style of the Japanese garment if it shows at the neck in a place not covered by a Japanese kimono. We find side by side in the same person a taste for Western music, which lives by expression, and a taste for Japanese music, which demands repression. Such discrepancies are present in every phase and aspect of modern Japanese life—in politics, food, living conditions, and transport. Creation is replaced by juxtaposition, synthesis by swiftness of transition. What to us appears chaotic is called by them a proof of their capacity to synthesise oriental and occidental cultures.

A Japanese to whom all this is pointed out will probably reply: "You do not understand us because we are so simple." I have heard these words—which frequently veil a claim to superiority in the language of humility—very often from the mouths of Japanese students unable or unwilling to satisfy the demands of a European university teacher. In the presence of conflicting theories they will, with few unforgotten exceptions, simply throw up their hands, resting content with the statement that authorities disagree, that for the time being, therefore, the question has to be shelved. Examination answers often contain a catalogue of such "opinions" instead of a solution of the problem, except in cases where a verbatim reproduction of the "opinion" of one professor is believed to be satisfactory.

The Japanese mind and soul, compared with ours, appear to lack a dimension. They resemble a plane or a system of planes; never attaining cubic volume, fullness, and depth. Are not their dwelling houses—here, as everywhere, the truest symbolic expressions of a nation's deepest urges—assemblages of planes rather than three-dimensional fabrics made out of space? Japanese walls and windows are in fact mere screens. The depth of the *tokonoma*, the domestic place of honour, has been reduced to a symbolic minimum. The two-dimensional nature of their painting and drawing was the first characteristic observed by Europeans. The same law seems to govern personal relations. Friendships, not only with foreigners, after having been established, often on the first contact, remain unchanged as they are, almost never gaining new ground, intensity, fullness, development.

The fact that Japanese seldom keep up intercourse with Europeans

4

in whom they are genuinely interested is often explained by their reluctance to undergo the strain imposed by Western conversation, quite apart from linguistic difficulties; they find it tiring to sustain intellectual effort, to change its directions and to participate in attempts to shape and reshape, formulate and reformulate, test and recast ideas and feelings, aims and standards. Emerson's visit to Carlyle for the first and last time after years of correspondence, silently seated by the fireside satisfied with their precious and brief presence together, appears to the Japanese as the ideal form of intercourse. Basho's famous *haiku* of the frog jumping into the old temple pond with a single splashing sound is to them another definite expression of final satisfaction.

The European mind is a battlefield where all spiritual and intellectual forces of the past daily resume their tragic fight; it recalls the legend of the warriors killed on the Catalaunian Fields and rising anew each night in order to continue their struggle. In such states of mind the Japanese take neither pride nor pleasure. To "settle" spirits is the chief aim of ritual; to "settle" things is the proper word for ruling a country. This race of warriors does not believe in the Heraclitean idea of war as the father of all things, and it has no place for the correlative idea of personality as the West understands it; for this is a structure hammered out in the unending struggle between man and his fate, mind and matter, the individual and his environment, the soul and her temptations, creator and chaos. It is the task of the personality to achieve unity out of conflicting elements, to reduce chaotic virtualities to form and order, to make a whole out of what seemed hopelessly disparate. The Japanese does not know this ambition. Buddhism has taught him, or has encouraged him in his tendency, to deny the very existence of an individual soul. To conceive of his own interior sphere of mind as an articulate, structured, self-creating mental fabric is an idea utterly alien to him. He does not feel an urge to make his ego a microcosmic image of the universe, to become god-like by shaping himself after a divine image. He does not wait for the decisive challenge that he must take up if his true self is to be realised. Life to him is not a substance which is to be given shape, form, order, but a force to be suffered patiently or to be received in one violent moment of fulfilment.

So there are two modes of existence for the Japanese. Either he yields to a motley set of natural instinct-like impulses, canalised in normal times into a system of customary rules of behaviour, but liable to break all bounds in arbitrary rudeness where the magic of ceremonial fails. Or he resolves to withdraw from this world by sacrificing his life on the battlefield, or by committing suicide, or by ascetic discipline which, he expects, will carry him to the realm of nought, or the "form of the formless", "the sound of the soundless". Choosing the first way, he will take his teaching from water that runs, clouds that move, algae that float, patiently obeying the interplay of forces of his environment. If he chooses the second way he will feel like an arrow shot by an archer stronger than himself towards a goal transcending this drab world of change and ambiguity.

Is it necessary to add the caution that such statements demand to be flavoured by some grains of salt? There are in Japan, ancient and modern, men and women from whom it would be impossible to withhold the title, "a personality"—men and women who are makers of their own character, who are governed by a personal style of life and able to mould from the evanescent complexity of feelings and volitions, thoughts and tastes, a fabric of crystalline beauty. No racial heritage seems to hinder the emergence of such personalities. But it is mainly in the border regions of Japanese life that we encounter such achievements: in the great monks who have left this world, and in the great courtesans and *geisha* who are living beyond the pale; and it is significant that in each case life means surrender, not fulfilment. It is in the style of their self-abandonment that they are granted a degree of self-determination denied to ordinary members of the human hive.

All ways in Japan lead to self-abandonment, and in each case the surrender of one's will appears to be performed with such wholehearted assent, and even joy, that we may ask whether the deepest urge of the men of this race is not a desire to disappear, to die, and thus to return to that maternal realm from which the individual emerges only in order to perish.

By one of the strangest paradoxes of human history, this race—loving the night, effacement, darkness—has come to believe in the sun-origin of their rulers and, finally, of the whole nation. Nothing is more alien to their souls than pure radiance and the blazing light that forces clarity and distinctness on everything. When the priest Mansei, early in the eighth century, compared this world to "the white wake behind a ship that has rowed away at dawn", he lent expression also to the profound longing of his race: *to return* to Nature's womb without leaving any other trace than a graceful ripple of fleeting foam.

3

The Crucible
of Nature

Here is a small country, scantily endowed by nature with arable land and mineral resources, separated from the eastern fringe of the Asian mainland by treacherous seas and mists; for more than two centuries closed of its own will to foreign intercourse almost entirely, after having incorporated into its life the great and dangerous gifts of late Chinese formalism and Indian quietism; before the middle of the nineteenth century with only rare, scrappy glimpses of experimental science; yet remaining alert and adaptable, vigorous and tenacious enough to resist, as the only non-European power of some magnitude, the impact of Western imperialism. Only a few decades after escaping by a narrow margin the danger of being made the object of foreign colonisation, this country vanquished with swift bold strokes the monarchies of China and Russia. After a few more decades of accelerated industrialisation it launched the venture to establish hegemony over the whole of East Asia and the seas and islands of the Western Pacific, in a struggle involving China, the British Commonwealth, and the United States, on the vastest theatre a war has ever been fought in, against fantastic odds. The price was paid in dire defeat; but while losing her empire Japan saved the essentials of what she calls her "national structure".

Compared with the rather young and for the most part chronically unstable Western "states", Japan seems to resemble a tree or a coral-reef rather than a man-made fabric. Her national anthem, *Kimigayo*, expresses the same idea in the wish that the reign of the emperors may last "until the pebbles of the river-bed have become rocks covered with moss"—slow irresistible growth pertaining to the order of mineral and vegetable processes.

It is not necessary to paint the development of this social organism in the pastel shades of a patriarchal idyll. It has been replete with conflict and dissension, cunning and violence; and the chronicles compiled by orders of the rulers of the Nara era leave no doubt that violence did not halt before the doors of monarchs deemed to be sacrosanct: some were murdered, some discarded, some banished. Few exerted political influence. They served more as priestly mediators than as actual rulers, in a world of intense strife, of heated factionalism and of ever active forces of self-destruction. Japan's claim to distinction rests not on an absence of pernicious forces but on the fact that throughout history they have been mastered.

Perhaps one can find for every single creation of the Japanese mind an equal, often a superior, counterpart in Western civilisation. But Japan is unique by virtue of the unparalleled continuity, homogeneity and plasticity of her political and cultural life over a range of centuries which in the West witnessed the greatness and decay of the Roman Empire, the migration of nations, the rise and fall of medieval hierarchies and Islamic empires, the formation of territorial states, the English, French, and Russian revolutions, and the threatening dawn of that Promethean civilisation that took the torch out of the hands of Greece.

Geography seems to have favoured the Japanese. Nothing appears to be more likely to produce uncommon degrees of unity and coherence than life on islands isolated by stormy and dangerous seas offering more hindrances than incentives to primitive navigation. Shielded for long periods from the disturbing impact of other races, yet under the ever-present menace of potential foreign invasion, such islands seem compelled by nature to give less weight to internal differences than to the needs of the social whole. However, neither Sicily nor Ireland, Crete nor Iceland, are famous for political success and social harmony.

Nor can the characteristics of Japanese society be explained by racial homogeneity, conceived of as natural endowment. The race has been formed in a crucible into which materials of very different origins have been thrown. The problem of the anthropological affinities and of the migratory past of the Japanese is far from having been solved. But most foreign students will be ready to admit that at least three main components can be distinguished with tolerable degrees of precision: Northern Mongols and other early inhabitants of North-East Asia, including some pre-Caucasians; Ainus, probably belonging to the Alpine race; and Malayo-Indonesians with strong Mediterranean affinities, but crossed with Southern Mongols and sometimes carrying slight admixtures of negroid blood acquired during their wanderings in the south east. Whoever studies the physiognomies of some dozens of contemporary Japanese thrown together by chance in a railway waiting-room or assembled (through the possibly no less irrational working of the entrance examination system) in a university classroom, will be first struck by their astonishing diversity of type. Perhaps the symptoms of a highly complex mixture are more visible today than in pre-modern times, when facial expression, demeanour and gesture were dominated by strong traditions prescribing uniformity of speech, looks, behaviour. For what we call a racial type appears to be largely the product of patterns of thought, feeling, action. Physiognomies are moulded as powerfully by these patterns as by anatomy.

By Japanese patriots, searching for a counterpart to the "nordic" ancestors fashionable in the thirties, the children of the sun were not seldom identified with a Tungusic people, who came from the northern mainland and conquered the islands of Japan two thousand odd years ago, incorporating the other races that lived there or entered the islands later. One cannot help observing that those north-east Asian tribes have nowhere else given any evidence of political ability, unlike the Normans whose role they are thought to have played in the Far East. They are thus of no avail in solving the problem of Japan's cohesive power.

It would be easier to find a remote counterpart to Norman

state-building in those South-East Asian tribes of probable Indonesian origin that are presumed to have spread from the Malay Peninsula, or from South China, into different regions of the Pacific under the rule of clans claiming descent from the Sun-God, or the War-God, and preserving their mythical genealogies as their most precious heirlooms. In Japan, as in England, an essentially alien dominating race has been blended with the conquered races so completely that today differences of descent bear almost no relation to political or social distinctions. But this new racial unity is due to political instinct or wisdom. It is not a *datum* but a *factum* of history. Nature has offered great advantages, but more remarkable than these are the ways in which state-building races have availed themselves of those vague invitations to greatness.

The tight-knit fabric of Japanese society is thus not a gift of "soil and blood". Nor is it due to far-sighted planning, deep thought, and action based on ideas. The Western mind is eminently architectonic; its urge is to give shape to the chaotic, to co-ordinate multiple elements that seem to defy attempts to unite them; it feels vanquished if it cannot plan and mould according to an ideal image of timeless value; even its worst dejections and scepticisms are those of a builder-mind. It would be absurd to call the Greek mind a tool-maker; but it was the Greek *techne*, a knowledge, device, almost a "knack", serving to do things better than by mere routine and tradition, which outlined most intellectual pursuits of the political architects of later Western and Central Europe.

The Japanese mind is, in this sense, un-technical. It does not believe in the efficiency of rational patterns; and what it achieves is more often than not incapable of generalisation and defies rational analysis.

The living constitution of the country—a thing that differs vastly from the written constitutions copied from Chinese or European books—does not resemble any Eastern or Western precedent. It embodies no definite system of rights and duties that cannot in certain circumstances be encroached upon or evaded. Ostensible and real authority are mostly wide apart. Delegation is practised to such a degree of diffusion that responsibility cannot be located with tolerable certainty. Monarchical, democratic and aristocratic elements are mixed so subtly as to make the body politic shine in every colour of the rainbow. The abstract concept of liberty seems to be absent, or to be pronounced with a distinctly foreign accent, but even plain disobedience is justified if it is a protest against an incompetent chief or an unreasonable demand. There are laws and courts of law modelled upon European systems, but it would be improper to make use of them in affairs of daily life. The perpetrators of political crimes may be deified without the State intervening. In every sphere of life decisions are made from case to case; and the term *decision* does not seem quite appropriate to a state of affairs where, on principle, everything remains fluid. A theory of public law taught for decades to thousands of future officials may suddenly be termed criminal. Nobody is allowed to stand on his *right;* and the task of the statesman appears to consist not in building up but in smoothing out and leaving all doors open.★

The course of history shows that this systematically unsystematic way of life has achieved notable results in the case of Japan. It could not be applied to other nations without leading to ruin and anarchy. The art of strategy and tactics has been defined as an "aggregate of makeshifts". No definition of the political wisdom of Japan could be more precise. Even the question whether Japan was or was not a theocracy had never been authoritatively settled before 1946—when the Emperor himself denied his divinity. Prince Ito, the maker of the Meiji Constitution, seems to have relegated the idea of a Japanese theocracy to the past; perhaps it was for this reason that his Commentaries on the Constitution

---

★ In this paragraph Singer's views are undoubtedly coloured very strongly by his recollection of political events during the 1930s. It would be wholly false to suggest that in Japan today "nobody is allowed to stand on his *right*." Indeed concepts of individual human rights are always stressed and accepted in education, in the press, and in political gatherings. Singer's reference to "a theory of public law taught for decades to thousands of future officials" applies to the works of Minobe Tatsukichi. (See footnote on page 28.) [Ed.]

were sometimes in danger of being put on the *index librorum prohibitorum*. But even the defenders of the most extreme claims to be ruled over by emperor-gods (a claim apparently never raised by the Emperor Meiji himself or his successors) failed to follow their idea to its logical conclusion—to reserve to a faculty of theology the interpretation and the teaching of Japanese public law. Nor did a single supporter of the divine character of the rulers rise in defence of the *Imperial Precepts to Soldiers and Sailors* (which clearly forbade the fighting forces from taking part in political life) when fanatical minorities of Army leaders forced the nation into the path of activist politics. Of many important phases of Japanese history throughout the ages it can be said that they were not willed by the legitimate holders of authority, but were just allowed to happen.

While the political structure of Japan appeared until yesterday as a rule of tradition hallowed by legend, spurred on by the illegal impulses of activist minorities, and tempered by remnants of a popular right of resistance (similar to that of the European Middle Ages), the economic life of Japan was always characterised by everlasting poverty, ennobled by the austere light of self-denying aesthetic cults and interspersed with luxurious citadels of wealth and over-refinement.

The Japanese language, so rich in synonyms, has no authentic word denoting "economy". *Keizai* refers to the politico-spiritual guidance of social life in general. During the Tokugawa period numerous tracts and essays were written on topical problems of monetary policy, agricultural progress, and business ethics, but the idea of a science dealing with supply and demand and their mutual adaptations seems not to have emerged before the introduction of Western political economy in the Meiji era. In this sphere the reception and assimilation of foreign methods of thinking and organising were obviously performed with more skill and common sense than in the field of constitutional law. But the great contributions of the Japanese economy to the political life of the nation were bought at an appalling price in poverty, distress, malnutrition, and lack of personal security. Hasty measures originating from emergency situations were allowed to remain in force long after basic conditions had been altered; and no new idea was produced which could claim to represent an original contribution to the solution of the economic and social problems of contemporary society. In this field, too, success was achieved in spite of, not because of, existing institutions. Here, too, the peculiarly Japanese note has been an uncommon degree of suffering, patience, toleration of abuses, rather than uncommon degrees of foresight, inventiveness, constructive power, or initiative.

If any Western nation had decided to impose similar burdens of restraint and want, drudgery and arbitrariness, its public life would have been constantly threatened with disruption and up-heaval. It is quite unlikely that political unity and continuity would have been preserved under such strains. If Japan endured them and even continued to grow and gain in political strength, the reason must be sought in a sphere that is more fundamental than the realm of political and economic institutions proper.

Offspring of rationalism and first cousins of machine-building, the most influential doctrines of the eighteenth and nineteenth centuries have dwelt upon what can be made, not upon what grows; on tools purposely devised, not on substances received or on limits set by nature; on societies formed for particular and rationalised ends, not on communities that resemble organic bodies of slow vegetative formation, which find their unity expressed in living symbols: a hearth, a god, a flag, a hero, or a dream. Such communities cannot be made at will. They belong to the borderland of nature and culture, landscape and history, *physis* and *nomos*; and instead of claiming them either for the realm of necessity or for that of freedom we should ask—if we try to understand the law of their formation—with Henri Bergson: what would nature do to make life possible for a being endowed with the capacity for intelligence, speech and free decision; no longer able to rely on invariable sets of instincts; not held together in the way the cells of an organism or the members of a hive are shaped into an imperious whole; but repeating in the sphere of conscious life and purposive behaviour the pattern of organic interdependence with similar success? The answer to this question is found in the archetype of small groups knit by usage of instinct-like power, hierarchically organised, fit for a virtual state of war, drawing strength from the belief in tribal gods inseparable from the life of the group; a primordial human society for which nature has furnished, as it were, a diagram that "vague and incomplete, corresponds, in the realm of reasonable and free activity, to what is, in the case of instinct, the clear-cut design of the ant-hill or the hive at the other terminal point of evolution."

If one dominant cause is to be found for the phenomenon of Japan's durability I should not hesitate to seek it in the fact that in the minutest detail of her way of life she has followed those hints of nature which Western nations have too often disregarded. The latter have given their allegiance to forces that invest life with a higher aim and a profounder impulse but are a source of great danger as long as man continues to plan his New City without consulting the soil that is to bear it.

The chapters that follow undertake to apply these ideas to the interpretation of the structural characteristics of Japanese society. They are based on observations made before the war. As I have not revisited the country, and as I have found in recent literature no evidence substantial enough to allow far-reaching inferences to be drawn, I have refrained from commenting on the reforms instituted in the wake of Japan's defeat and occupation. Here and there I have changed the present tense of my first draft into the past; but I have not been pedantic about this. For I am still inclined to think that, in spite of legislative changes which may in the long run affect some social relations, the fundamental pattern that has grown through centuries, following its own organic logic, will not be readily changed in a political environment of great instability. If I should be mistaken Japan will have ceased to be the nation I have known, and my account will record a closed chapter of some memorable centuries of social history.

If on the other hand my analysis should prove correct, the

reader anxious, for good reasons, to find guarantees for peace in the Pacific need not necessarily be alarmed by the incongruity of what is here described with what is usually regarded as pre-requisites of the "Good Life". Experience has shown that neither the emancipation of women nor the reduction of tenant farming are sure guarantees of peace; and that non-party governments are not necessarily warlike. During her so-called "feudal" past covering twelve centuries Japan has made attacks only twice on the Asiatic mainland, in the seventh and sixteenth centuries; and in both cases they were quickly abandoned after a first taste of what such ventures implied. This is too slender a basis for prediction, but it goes far to strengthen the belief that reforms, though useful and not to be discredited, are of themselves neither sufficient nor necessary conditions of peaceful behaviour. There is more than one type of good life; and in the case of a nation so sensitive as Japan to atmospheric changes, the general climate of international relations will be of greater importance than legal reforms in spheres which according to Japanese tradition are largely governed by custom.

4

The Law of
Harmonious Flow

THE AXIOM

The life of every society can be considered under two aspects: as a process or as a product. Our attention may be focused on the way in which human actions and attitudes are made to fit into flexible patterns of limited durability; or we may judge the fabric emerging from this flux. Japanese society seems to be built upon the axiom that the first of these viewpoints must be dominant.

With a precision and finality extremely rare, if ever paralleled, in the formative stages of other societies, Prince Shotoku, the saint-founder of the Japanese state, has struck the key-note of all Japanese life in the first article of the Code of State Ethics promulgated in the seventh century A.D.

"Harmony is to be valued, and an avoidance of wanton opposition to be honoured. All persons are influenced by class-feelings, and there are few who are intelligent. Hence there are some who disobey their lords and fathers or who maintain feuds with the neighbouring villages. But when those above are harmonious and those below are friendly, and there is concord in the discussion of business, right views of things spontaneously gain acceptance. Then what is there that cannot be accomplished?"

These precepts echo early Chinese teachings; the phenomenon that deserves our attention is the way in which they have been incorporated in the life of everyday Japan, where they seem to have acquired the force of a biological instinct, serving the ends of a human society that aspires to rival in cohesive power the societies of bees and ants.

To make the stream of human intercourse flow gently is the supreme goal here. Nobody is allowed to stand on his own right, much less fight for it. Conflicts must be submitted for mediation and are solved by compromise. Justice is praised, but its pursuit is deemed inappropriate if the peace of the community is thereby threatened. To avoid friction seems to be more important than to eradicate evil. One of the articles of the *Legacy of Ieyasu* says: "The law may upset reason, but reason may never upset the law . . . The law may be used to confound reason, but reason must certainly not be used to overthrow the law." According to another article it is forbidden to alter "a faulty regulation if, through inadvertency, it has been allowed to remain in force during fifty years."[1] Continuity and wont are of greater importance than what is right and just. There is no idea more alien to this mode of life than the Heraclitean teaching that war is the father of all things.

The ways of Westerners in their daily life appear intolerably harsh to the Japanese; they see in the intercourse even of those Westerners who are on friendly terms a perpetual giving and taking of blows and shocks; either they do not perceive the sparks that spring from such clashes of personality and will, or the frictions are deemed too high a price for what is achieved in these antagonistic ways. Perhaps they are wise in not following us here: if their societies allowed the same measure of actual and virtual strife that is to us a constant stimulus of life, their aptitude for extremes in love and hate, revenge and insult, would keep their social structure in danger of being rocked by an unending series of emotional eruptions, tidal waves, and 'quakes. Wherever social intercourse is not standardised according to immemorial custom and canalised in a network of ceremonial rites, the Japanese— probably all Eastern nations—are likely to act and speak with dangerous arbitrariness and discourtesy. Where the quasi-magical force of rite and custom prevails, the give and take, address and reply, the warp of daily life, assume the harmonious aspects of a self-regulated organic process.

EXPERIENCES

The sacrifices demanded by this way of life will appear to any Westerner too great to make its adoption desirable. But to a student of man and of his societies it is most illuminating to enter for a shorter or longer period the current of this alien form of life with an open mind. He will probably have been told by discriminating Japanese friends that he should continue to regulate his behaviour according to Western standards: most Japanese would consider a foreigner acting in Japanese style not less ridiculous than a mammal that would adopt the manners of a bird or fish. But if the foreigner continues to follow this excellent advice he will soon find himself in a state of disagreeable isolation —save for the company of other, easily bored, foreigners and of rather unattractive Japanese adepts of indiscriminate Westernisation. Continuously hurting and being hurt—without intention in either case—and he will remain a source of chronic wonder and anxiety to his environment, and often experience great difficulties in solving the simplest problems of daily existence.

Let him, experimentally but unreservedly, behave according to Japanese custom, and he will instantly feel what a cell endowed with rudiments of human sensibility must be supposed to feel in a well-coordinated body. There is a bewildering number of conventions and taboos, in various degrees of unintelligibility; if these are mastered and observed, life becomes singularly easy and entrancing. Every attitude is requited in a nicely predictable way, act calling forth act according to an accepted pattern, every detail of which is fitted into the whole of the situation with the precision of a design for a piece of elaborate machinery. The main objection against undesirable forms of human behaviour is here termed *muri*; which may mean: an unreasonable attitude, disregard of custom and precedent, use of violence or violation of a cosmic law. One meaning shades off into the other without hard and fast demarcation lines.

NATURAL AND SOCIAL LAW

This way of amalgamating natural law and social convention will appear archaic and unacceptable to a Westerner; who may feel himself far above a level on which the breach of etiquette, a sin against nature, or a deviation from the path of reason are considered to be closely akin, if not identical. But if he candidly observes his own reactions in this alien element he will discover that his subconscious mind has remained subject to similar impulses. If he receives a letter written in a European language by a Japanese, in which the Western rules of politeness are disregarded, or if he hears a Japanese (or, *a fortiori*, a Chinese) make the appropriate noises prescribed by Far Eastern custom when eating, or rather drinking, soup, he will more or less distinctly feel offended, helpless, or at least disagreeably puzzled; and he will perhaps observe in himself a quasi-instinctive indignation emerging from his unconscious. Such reactions lend great force to Bergson's theory that life, when endowing man with intelligence and thus exposing this new kind of organism to disintegrating forces of dangerous virtualities, has enabled him to replace the invariable system of animal instincts by a close-meshed network of habits and customs more plastic than their zoological counterparts, but assimilated to them in the human mind in such a way that "what is done" assumes the character of "what must happen".

In Japan this network of ceremonial forms is not only more closely knit than in the modern societies of the West, but without these forms life would lose its meaning. Here, to do "what is done" not only substantiates one's claim to belong to a certain class or to evoke certain reactions from other men; it is often the only way of making oneself understandable.

A seasonal present made to one's gardener, if not wrapped up in the prescribed manner and with the appropriate ideograms written on the enveloping paper, would be a riddle but not the

5

customary gift; the foreigner need not be surprised if it is not properly acknowledged with thanks in the usual style. Not to take off one's greatcoat before entering the vestibule of a Japanese house would put into a most perplexing situation the maid who opens the door: how should she deal with a stranger acting in such an unpardonable manner towards her master?* The Japanese eagerness to copy minutely, even pedantically, every detail observed in foreign countries must be largely the outcome of such situations: they may remember the havoc inflicted on their feelings by foreigners displaying a genial indifference to the ways of life that appear trivial or unreasonable to the alien but make life intelligible, significant and worth living to the "natives". To know these rules and to act upon them deftly and unerringly is called *umai*; which means: nice, sweet, tasting well, skilful, successful.

UNCONSCIOUSNESS

The ultimate purpose of this system of ritual-like customs seems to be the transformation of everyday life into a quiet stream, reflecting a state of mind that is close to unconsciousness: things are happening as in a pleasant dream, where every event is the fulfilment of a latent wish. Servant girls are talking to one another in the language of princesses; a bus-conductor will excuse himself for having made the passengers wait, although the car starts with mathematical precision; the politest of guests, when parting, will apologise for having been very rude. No writer has described the charm of this way of life better than Lafcadio Hearn. "It is like a dream in which people greet us exactly as we like to be greeted, and say to us all that we like to hear, and do for us all that we wish to have done—people moving soundlessly through spaces of perfect repose, all bathed in a vapoury light."[2]

The dream will lift at last, "like those vapours of spring which lend preternatural loveliness to a Japanese landscape in the fore-

---

* Not many Japanese houses today would have their doors opened by a maid. But it is still good manners to remove one's overcoat before ringing the bell. [Ed.]

noon of radiant days." Dark powers thinly veiled will brusquely become visible, corrosive influences will not fail to do their saddening work, appearances and reality will diverge. But this awakening, recalling Prospero's *Epilogue*, does not detract from the magical charm of the dream as long as it was dreamt, nor from the value of a style of life which shapes out of this world of change, squalor and pettiness a realm of light and sweetness, harmonious flow and persistent gentleness.

The most characteristic enjoyments of the Japanese are governed by this law. What matters most in the style of the tea ceremony as well as of archery is the realisation of a quasi-somnambulist degree of unconsciousness; only if the performer can rely on a pattern of senso-motoric coordination so deeply ingrained that no phase of the performance requires cerebral intervention, is true mastery attained. The master-archer will hit the centre of his customary target in complete darkness; but the achievement of the hit is relatively unimportant compared with the noble, detached attitude, the unerring (because non-conscious) grace and power of his movements.* Consciousness is restricted to the narrowest sphere compatible with biological needs and economic conditions. It is never allowed to dominate; where it endangers the interplay of primordial instincts it is ruthlessly discarded; even where it is allowed to function, little value accrues to it: the Japanese seem to consider it as a *pudendum* rather than a source of pride.

So Japanese life appears to be always ready to fall back into the dreamy torpor of vegetative existence, firmly rooted in the ground, irresistibly drawn to the light by an involuntary heliotropism, persevering by yielding to the cosmic rhythm of seasonal change. There are some remnants of animal worship or animal

* Eugen Herrigel's book, *Zen in the Art of Archery* (London, Routledge and Kegan Paul, 1953) was in its first form a lecture delivered by Herr Herrigel to the German-Japanese Society in Berlin in 1936. It also appeared in the magazine *Nippon*. It is perhaps on this source that Singer depends for his description of the Master-archer. However, it is worth noting that Herrigel lived at Sendai for a period, and studied archery there. It is likely, therefore, that Singer knew him at that time. [Ed.]

totemism concerning dogs and crabs, foxes and monkeys, wolves, bears, and some birds, but they appear to have become mere shadows at an early time. Of higher rank and more persisting power are the cherry tree, the rice ear, the pine tree and other plants. This swiftest of races worships what is immobile—a tree, but also a rock; the most of tenacious races admires what is easily scattered by the lightest wind: one Imperial ancestress is the Goddess of the Falling Flowers.

THE RURAL INHERITANCE

The urge to be submerged in a sea of unconsciousness is deeply in harmony with the rustic affinities of the Japanese. Compared not only with mediterranean antiquity and medieval and modern West and Central Europe, but also with ancient China and Babylon, Japan is a distinctly non-urban country. There have been populous capitals, growing around the Imperial Household or around the castle of the Suzerain-Shogun, and there has been a small number of mercantile settlements which attained city status in minor degrees of autonomy and self-defence. But what characterises Japanese social history more than any other single trait is the absence of those many strong-willed, competitive, urban units in which Western civilisation found the source of its inspiration and its truest guardians.

This lack of cities in the proper sense cannot be explained by the geographical nature of a country which has so much in common with the classical countries of city life. The contrast with Greece is the more striking as Japan, too, seems to have been conquered in her formative stages by several waves of cognate warrior tribes, waves which in many respects remind us of the invasions of archaic Greece by Ionians, Aeolians and Dorians. In Japan, however, no heroic stand seems to have been made by clans determined to resist the invader; leaving their rural settlements, withdrawing to walled places of refuge, forming there a new kind of political life by throwing their tribal and gentilitial rules of social life into a melting pot from which thus emerged a new Law of the City. Nor do we find in later epochs of Japanese history, which in some important respects resemble the European Middle Ages, free corporations of men bound together by oath, able to throw off the yoke of imposed authorities, and to support their claims to freedom by the bravery of their own armies. Japanese cities up to the threshold of the Meiji era remain, with insignificant exceptions, mere irradiations of the life of a court, or mere agglomerations of traders without political will.

It is for these reasons that freedom is a plant without strong roots in Japanese history. There is a corresponding absence of almost everything the City has contributed to the social and political life of Europe; for most of these are gifts of the *agora*, the *forum*, the market place.

The concept of public affairs being discussed among equals in the open air, in clear outline, everyone assuming responsibility for his own words; the value of the spoken word arising from such debates; the habit of competing for power by peaceful means, by persuasion; the joy of attacking, and of defending oneself, ably and brilliantly; the growing together in common action and counsel of a new body politic not cemented by tribal or gentilitial ties; the replacing of patriarchal and feudal obligations and rights by new relationships, man-made but claiming the dignity of ancient law rooted in nature and mirroring the order of the universe; finally and supremely, the emergence of a new form of life centred in the creative and critical powers of mind, continually shaping and reshaping the legacy of the past according to the voice of the *forum internum*, giving birth to new sights on world and man, more ingenious and more deeply fraught with dangers than the slow plant-like growth of rural customs and organs—all this, with few exceptions, was absent from old Japan. And modern Japan often suffered from well-intentioned but somewhat hasty attempts at introducing Western institutions, which have their foundations deep in the soil of city life but are likely to lead a precarious and unstable life in a country whose traditions know nothing of citizens driving away their kings, counts, bishops or tyrants, insisting upon making their own laws and willing to die for their new freedom. Even Osaka, the nearest approximation to a self-governing city of traders, preferred to employ mercenaries to fight for it.

RUSTIC TRAITS

The most persistent, and some of the most valuable, features of Japanese society, even in our own day, are legacies of rural life. The best physiognomies often resemble certain ancient Roman figures which in spite of their urbanity betray a peasant origin. "Even in the town you will find the countryside" is a Japanese saying of great truth. To prefer silence to talking, to be suspicious of cleverness; to accept tradition without questioning; to suffer disaster without dismay, silently building anew what nature or man has destroyed; to be closely observant of what the neighbour does, or omits to do; to view life as a continual giving and taking, sunshine and rainfall, seasonal rhythm and earth-bound toil— these are distinctive traits of the village only slightly modified by life in the vast urban agglomerations of contemporary Japan.

The town-dweller who has severed the navel-cord of his rural origins is apt to become unstable, rude and lawless. He may try to outshine the courtiers, like the classical citizen of old Kyoto, by spending most of his income on beautiful clothes; or, like the Yedokko, the child of old Tokyo, he may try to out-herod Herod in toughness, generosity and truculence.★ In modern Japan the history of municipal administration was largely a chronicle of corruption and bribery, often following a pattern all too familiar in the West. The amorphous character of Tokyo's streets, except in the immediate neighbourhood of the old Shogun's castle (now the Imperial Palace), is symbolic of the true nature of the Japanese city, a cluster of villages grown to immoderate dimensions.

★ A kind of "Pearly King" or "knocking 'em on the Old Kent Road" Cockney character has grown up round the image of the man born and bred in downtown Yedo (Tokyo), the Yedokko (lit. "child of Yedo"). [Ed.]

LAWS

It is this rural physiognomy of Japan which makes law in the Western sense, a product of ancient Greece and Rome, appear as a strange guest of uncertain authority in modern Japan. From an early age imperial edicts have been issued, breathing the spirit of the classical Chinese tradition, according to which the monarch guides the realm (*ten-ka*, "what is under heaven") more through his example and his quasi-magical virtue than by abstract norms that can be enforced by proper administrative organs. Chinese codes of law were introduced from the Nara era; but although later monarchs modified them to fit into the framework of Japanese society, their applicability to actual conditions remained problematical. During the Kamakura epoch the Hojo regents produced an excellent code of indigenous feudal law, superimposed on customary law, which continued to govern social life. The Hojo code, being intended to serve the Shogun's supreme court at Kamakura, remained unpublished until the later phase of the Tokugawa period. The House Laws of the Tokugawa Shoguns were also kept as treasured secrets of the ruling house, full of political and administrative wisdom but resembling a list of political maxims more than a system of law.

The only Chinese school of thought that has left no clear mark in Japanese literature and ethical theory is the school of the "legalists", who advised the ruler to rely on a well-defined set of laws, rewards, and punishments, instead of clinging to the classical Chinese doctrine of moral rule by exemplary conduct on the part of the ruler. During the early Meiji era codes of law modelled on those of Europe were compiled, in order to remove objections of foreign powers to Japan's attaining the status of an independent modern state free from foreign enclaves of consular jurisdiction. But according to pre-war observations it was considered, except perhaps within the world of big business, almost indecent to go to court. If a marriage is to be dissolved, an employee dismissed, an agreement interpreted, the proper way is to have a "talk" and, if this is unsuccessful, to accept mediation by a go-between or a common friend.

A settlement, in order to be found satisfactory, has to take into account more than the rights and duties stipulated in a contract. The whole situation of all parties concerned has to be considered— the former relations between the litigants, their relative wealth or poverty, power and social standing, and above all the peace of the community of which they are members. Law has not yet emerged from the stream of common life as a sphere of its own, opposing to the fluidity and many-sidedness of common life an abstract form, rational, hard and lucid like a crystal, objective and implacable. Between law and custom, habit and convention, order of nature and order of reason, natural inclination and social duty, no rigid demarcation lines are drawn. Everything remains contingent on circumstances, subject to swift transition.

The Japanese are averse to committing themselves to rules that, though beautiful and reasonable in themselves, may prove harmful to the peaceful flow of social life by introducing into this ever-changing element factors of excessive intellectual rigidity and harshness. They are equally opposed to allowing personal self-assertion and self-regard—standing on one's rights and fighting for one's sphere of "legally protected interests"—to obstruct the smooth flow of customary intercourse. Properly speaking, there are no "subjective rights" possible in a community where the demands of its harmonious self-adjustment take precedence over any other value.

This does not imply, as some rash Western writers seem to assume, that the Japanese submits blindly and patiently to "constituted authority". Every second page of Japanese history tells of acts against such men in authority as were deemed to govern or administer the country contrary to the welfare of the whole community: acts of resistance, rebellion, assassination, which are not only condoned but also often praised and rewarded. Every resident of Japan knows that neither a public office nor a business nor household can be administered contrary to the feelings of the staff members. As in every well-knit community an unwritten insurrection is behind the façade of placid submissiveness; a right founded, it is true, not on the concept of personality but of the whole having precedence over the best-grounded right of any member.

The Japanese is not by virtue of his nature impersonal or disposed to set little store by his personal interests, aims and rights. He does not lack individuality, nor does he conceal it wherever the social pattern does not interfere. The warriors of the *Heike Monogatari*, at the peak of the feudal age, vaunt themselves not less vigorously than Homeric heroes; and no great saint has ever said "I" with the same monumental emphasis as Nichiren, the most Japanese among the great Japanese monks and sect-founders.★ The various poets of the Heian era are characterised, in the preface of the *Kokinshu*, with an astonishing wealth of subtle distinctions; and the *Diary* of Murasaki Shikibu draws portraits of her companion court ladies with a sense for what is individual, unique, inimitable, that in the West did not exist until the threshold of the modern age.

The significant fact is not the absence of individuality, of the desire to make it felt and appreciated, but the hypnotic spell cast by the demands of "natural society" whenever the harmonious flow of social life is liable to be endangered. As soon as this situation arises, these people need no admonition from philosophic moralists or political propaganda: a force irresistible and blind seems to emerge instantaneously, bending them with the power of an instinct in the direction desired by the human anthill. Inclinations, friendships, enterprises, studies are abandoned, without any struggle or deliberation, in obedience to that "constant force of direction that is to the soul what gravity is to bodies", assuring the cohesion of the group by inclining individual wills in the same direction and thus creating "an order dictated by impersonal requirements".³ Only a fatalistic, sadly enjoyed

★ Whether or not Nichiren (1222–1282) was "the most Japanese", he was beyond doubt the greatest nationalist among the great Japanese religious figures. He was also, as Singer suggests, aggressively self-assured and egotistical. He is well remembered for his declaration: "I will be the pillar of Japan. I will be the eyes of Japan. I will be the great vessel of Japan." [Ed.]

shikata ga nai ("this cannot be helped") testifies that there is no pre-ordained harmony between the whole and its parts.

NOTES

1 A. L. Sadler, *The Maker of Modern Japan; the Life of Tokugawa Ieyasu*, London, 1937, p. 392.
2 Lafcadio Hearn, *Japan, An Interpretation*, London, 1904, pp. 18–19.
3 Henri Bergson, *The Two Sources of Morality and Wisdom*, London, 1935, p. 226.

5

The Law of
Small Numbers

THE SMALL GROUP

Japan is a nation far more populous than Great Britain or France; but the structure and the political physiognomy of the country have retained the characteristics of a small group of men, characteristics such as are likely to arise from neighbourhood, kinship, or teamwork. The modern mind nurtured on sciences mainly concerned with quantities, and all too accustomed to the use of mechanical magnifiers, likes to assume that between the behaviour of small and big things there is no difference—a typical layman's misunderstanding, for the true mathematician and physicist know very well that the realms of the small and the great often obey quite different rules. In social life the difference is profound and all-pervading.

Only in small groups do we feel spontaneously prompted to act in solidarity, and to pronounce the shibboleth "we" without hesitation. Such attitudes may be transferred to greater units in the wake of spiritual and political revolutions, but the result will remain precarious. Modern states are more apt to disintegrate than the number and strength of unifying factors would suggest. A shared heritage of law, of education, of historical experience, of language and cult, of interests and animosities, may provide large nations with strong ligaments; but these cannot make up for the lack of that feeling of unconditional connectedness, fateful oneness, which characterises the small group.

A growing society desirous of overcoming this "hiatus" can

proceed on two lines. It can fashion new ties after the image of those binding small societies; or it can buttress the institutional framework appropriate to large-scale groups, by developing an intricate system of small society supports. Both ways have been followed by Japan.

Unlike Europeans, whose minds have been moulded by the Greek *agora,* the Roman *forum,* the medieval guild-halls and modern parliaments, the Catholic Church, the Holy Roman Empire, or the several Socialist Internationals, the Japanese seem to harbour an instinctive antipathy towards large-scale associations. They feel uneasy in large conferences, preferring man-to-man talks in which they can show their natural skill and feel at home. To gather professors of different universities in regular professional meetings is a rather difficult affair; for the universities seem to retain some of the traits of feudal baronies. In politics and administration local ties are still of importance. If two key ministers come from the same province, this is considered as a good omen of their readiness to cooperate.

THE ARMY

The frailty of large-scale institutions in Japan is well illustrated by the threatened decay of army discipline that became apparent in the course of the so-called Showa revolution of the 'thirties. Younger officers set their will against that of their seniors; parts of the Tokyo garrison were used for seditious purposes; high-ranking officers were assassinated; the officer corps seemed on the verge of breaking up into a number of factions; and the *Imperial Precepts to the Soldiers and Sailors* given by the Meiji Emperor were patently disregarded.★

These phenomena would have been strange in any country, and they stood out in sharp contrast to the social discipline of

★ Singer refers here to the sensational insurrection of part of the Tokyo garrison led by young officers, on 26th February 1936. The best account in the English language to date (1972) that I have seen is by Ben-Ami Shillony, "The February 26 Affair: Politics of a Military Insurrection", in George M. Wilson, *Crisis Politics in Prewar Japan*, Tokyo, Sophia University, 1970, pp. 25–50. [Ed.]

which Japan had been boasting. They became explicable as a result of the waning influence of small-scale groups that had dominated the fighting services since their formation seventy years earlier. The army and navy were built up from very small beginnings patiently and persistently under the guidance, or even rule, of two groups of men—the army by the survivors of the Choshu *han*, the navy by the survivors of the Satsuma *han*. The term *han* is generally translated by the word "clan"; an almost ineradicable nuisance, for the *han* was not a group of families united by the belief in descent from a common ancestor and by unconditional duty to mutual support in blood-feuds. The word denoted a small territorial political organisation, a barony, as Professor Asakawa proposes to call it, governed by the local *daimyo*, formally a liegeman of the Tokugawa suzerain, in fact—within his territory—an autocratic monarch in miniature administering his land with the aid of *samurai* retainers. When this quasi-feudal structure was abolished early in the Meiji era, the retainers and their families remained united to their former lords by feelings of personal gratitude and traditional allegiance, and these bonds were nowhere stronger than in the Choshu and Satsuma baronies, whose retainers undertook to reconstruct the fighting forces and continued to produce all the leading officers of those forces for half a century.

As long as these personal allegiances and dependencies were still alive, the discipline of the army was beyond question. It was only after the men who had served their lords under the Tokugawa regime had died out and personal ties had gradually lost strength that those astonishing breaches of discipline, in the 'thirties, could occur. More rationalised types of discipline and subordination, imported from the West, do not appear to have developed, as yet, that cohesive force once furnished by the personal bond between lord and retainer, patrimonial ruler and hereditary officer-official. It is not easy to instil in the Japanese loyalties of an abstract order: to an idea, a creed, an order, a law, valid for practically unlimited aggregations.

POLITICAL PARTIES

The same difficulties seemed to beset, before the war, the way of political parties and the development of parliamentary methods. Japanese parties were not held together by programmes, convictions, ideas. To the foreign observer they appeared as mere aggregates of small factions of followers of one public figure (who often remained hidden "behind a curtain"). Loosely built up by ambitious aristocrats or demogogic adventurers, they were liable to split up as soon as two leading men were unable to compose their differences, which were possibly of a quite personal nature. These impressions are confirmed by the most venerable and most intrepid of Japanese politicians, Ozaki Yukio, a member of the Diet since its inauguration.*

"Here in the Orient", Ozaki wrote in 1917, "we have had political factions but no political party. A political party is an association of people having for its exclusive object the discussion of public affairs of state and the enforcement of their views thereon. But when political parties are transplanted into the East, they at once partake of the nature of factions, pursuing private and personal interests, instead of the interests of the State—as witnessed by the fact of their joining hands in turn with the clan cliques or using the construction of railways, ports and harbours, schools, etc., as a means for extending party influence. Besides, the customs and usages of feudal times are so deeply impressed upon the minds of men here that even the idea of political parties, as it enters the brains of our countrymen, is influenced by feudal notions. Such being the case, even political parties, which

* Ozaki Yukio (1858–1954) achieved a record of parliamentary membership probably unequalled anywhere. Elected to the House of Representatives in Japan's first general election, in 1890, he was re-elected on twenty-three consecutive occasions. Minister of Education in 1898, Mayor of Tokyo in 1908, and Minister of Justice in 1915, Ozaki survived to sit in the post-war Diet under the new Constitution. Inevitably, he was known in later years by the title, "Father of Parliamentary Politics". [Ed.]

should be based and dissolved solely on principles and political views, are really affairs of personal connections and sentiments, the relations between the leader and the members of a party being similar to those which subsisted between a feudal lord and his liegemen."

Ozaki added:

"It is small wonder that political parties, as well as other institutions and bodies, should have failed to achieve any marked development. At this rate of progress, the realisation of a true constitutional government seems to lie in the dim and distant future."[1]

The weaknesses discussed here were to be found not only in the main central parties, Seiyukai and Minseito, which originated in aristocratic factions tied by personal bonds and were finally held together mainly by party financiers of great skill, but also in the revolutionary parties of the extreme right and left. Writing in the 'thirties, a leading socialist, the late Mr Mogi, observed:

"Party membership is a very vague term, as applied to Japan. The two main party headquarters have registers of their members throughout the country, but these lists consist of a heterogeneous collection of people who can be relied upon to do odd jobs for the party in return for a proper reward, people who for one reason or other have voted Minseito or Seiyukai as the case may be in this or that election, and only relatively few who have consistently given support to one or other of the parties and regularly expounded its policies in the constituency. Apparently, too, there is no regular subscription, or, for that matter, any regular or uniform obligation of any kind, imposed on these so-called "members". In the constituencies themselves it is well known that active political workers change their party incessantly, and what is the most astonishing thing of all is that numbers of people are registered as members of, and act for, both parties simultaneously. . . . The main lines of organisation are the same even in proletarian parties, although, of course, some funds are drawn from trade unions and some from small contributions of active members. Even in these parties, however, there is a tendency to seek out wealthy patrons, and it is just this system of patronage which, on the one hand, has discredited the political parties with the public and, on the other, militated against the growth among them of any genuine political principle or independence of spirit."[2]

PUBLIC AND PRIVATE SERVANTS

The handling of vast numbers of men was no new problem in modern Japan. The armies employed in the great internal wars of the sixteenth century were probably larger than any European forces engaged in battles of that period, and the handling of those masses was—according to the judgement of Professor James Murdoch—equal, if not superior to, Western generalship.[3] Bureaucracy was an earlier growth in Japan than in Western or Central Europe during the Middle Ages. Feudal oaths of allegiance were administered in writing. After a battle the warrior made a written report of his actions, supported by witnesses. This could serve as a documentary basis of recompense and acknowledgment.[4] Even today, however, Japanese bureaucracy is characterised by a much greater freedom from mechanised discipline, abstract and universal rules and rigid unification than most Western counterparts. Every ministry seems to move according to its own house traditions, conserving a large measure of quasi-medieval corporative autonomy. There is a kind of unwritten corporation law stronger than cabinet decisions or the will of a Minister of State. Woe to any chief who would dare to disregard such traditions!

An official in a Government department or institution will claim a good deal of freedom in carrying out general instructions; if he should be interfered with by his superior in the details of his duties, the chief will soon learn that he has violated an important unwritten law of the country. There will usually be no strike (although the history of the Foreign Office knows instances of such forms of resistance) but work will be carried out in such an unpleasant way that the chief will prefer to change his practice.

The same conditions prevail in private households. A servant expects the master of the house to give general ideas on how he wants the household to be run. The execution must be left to the group of servants, one of whom will be in general charge. To choose a second or third servant without consulting, or against the advice of, the first will produce such morose and sluggish demeanour and such unsatisfactory ways of carrying out orders that the "tyrant" will soon desist from treating human beings as if they were cogs in a bureaucratic machine. A cook allowed to work according to his own discretion, within the general frame indicated by the master, will do his (or her) best, for his ambition is usually great. If he is ordered about too closely, he (or she) is likely to produce a caricature of what the master intended.

AVERSION TO MECHANISATION

These conditions may lead to what the Western observer considers frequently as a loss in technical efficiency. Objectives are attained with less precision, but the stifling results of mechanised unification are avoided. The public, as well as the private, servant wants to feel that he is a living being serving within a living organism, exercising a reasonable amount of initiative and freedom to execute orders in a way compatible with varying circumstances.

The servant, before the war, was generally paid very little, received very plain food and was lodged very poorly. But he was not a mere number; and if he worked for a family his status was very similar to that of a member of the family. His future was assured, within certain limits imposed by "conditions", as long as the household continued to exist. He was scolded for his shortcomings only in a case of gross misdemeanour, like the children of the house; otherwise he would be apt to reply that the fault was with the master who had decided to engage him: being the master he was supposed to be much superior in wisdom and

6

discrimination; in choosing just this servant he had acquired his shortcomings together with his abilities.

If the servant or the worker is dismissed, he is entitled to receive compensation even if he should happen to be a strike-leader. On the other hand, the chief, master, or officer has to act as adviser and helper to his subordinates in case of need or trouble. The officer in charge of a company, the teacher in an elementary school, is looked upon as the pillar of the family to which the soldiers in the company or the children in the class belong. To this extent the spirit of the small group has been conserved even in those larger associations which according to Western practice are allowed to be "run" on the principle of abstract regulation.

The Japanese aversion to all excesses of the mechanisation of human behaviour seems to account for the curious fact that the thoroughly German-trained army did not adopt the Prussian practice of marching in step when passing through the streets of a city. To make Japanese students read in perfect unison is extremely difficult. When the Takarazuka Ballet visited the United States their success was marred by the fact that their legs could not be made to swing in those machine-like patterns so pleasing to the freedom-loving theatre-goers of the Western world.

AGE GROUPS

It would be only a slight exaggeration to say that the smooth flux of ordinary Japanese life has in the past been secured not because of, but in spite of, the vast machinery built upon Western models: its true strength does not reside in the rationalised perfection of its mammoth organisations, but in the dense tissue of small society relationships supporting those vast superstructures and infusing their living substance into the framework of the Leviathan.

Some of these relationships are well in evidence: groupings on the principle of consanguinity or of neighbourhood. Of equal importance are ties binding men (much more rarely women) of the same age. Such age-classes are a phenomenon familiar to every student of primitive societies. In modern Western life there are only few traces of such groupings left, the origins of which seem to go back to times anterior to the formation of patriarchal families. Their survival in Japan is one of the most characteristic marks of the retentive power of the Japanese.

Such age groups are most easily observed in the village. An American writer who shared the life of villagers in Kyushu for one year has stated: " 'Boya' and men of the same age are close friends, those of the same age being called *donen*."[5] The Young Men's Associations of the countryside, although organisations built up for certain specific ends, seemed to retain some features of primitive age-classes, with their life centred in a men's hall.

First-year students in the pre-war *Kotogakko* (Higher School), generally aged seventeen to twenty, had to undergo rites which appear to perpetuate the initiation ceremonies of very early times. There were nightly excursions to graveyards and other haunted places, with terrifying mock-apparitions and other tests of courage. There were nightly round-dances of a quite archaic type performed in the dormitories by class-mates stripped to the waist, with hands laid on the shoulders of their neighbours, singing and going round and finally reeling in a kind of fraternalising ecstasy and thus welding young men of very different origin and often great natural shyness into an indissoluble whole. More than one of them has told me that he felt forlorn and homesick until he had danced what is called the *sturm* ("tempest", "storm") for the first time.*

* The *Kotogakko* (Higher School) no longer exists. I can fully confirm, from my own observations, the validity of Singer's comments on the ethos of Dormitory life. The "storms" were a notable feature of those institutions. Singer is correct, too, in his next paragraph when he stresses the importance of the ties binding class age groups at Higher Colleges. In particular, those who attended the pre-war First Higher School and Second Higher School (at Sendai, where Singer taught) maintained in later life school friendships of considerable political significance; since those attending these Higher Schools were an intellectual élite and often progressed, by way of Tokyo Imperial University, to responsible positions of authority in politics, big business, the academic world, and metropolitan journalism. The English "old school tie" is a pale, unimportant, phenomenon by comparison with the Higher School Old Boy Network. [Ed.]

It is said that nothing in Japanese life equals in binding force the ties uniting the class-mates of a *Kotogakko*. Every graduate seems to be compelled by custom to assist his former class-mates in any emergency, with a readiness not only equal but also often superior to that due to members of his own family. It was probably the close symbiosis in which these young men lived, far from the muddy stream of worldly affairs, with a fair dose of leisure to talk, to read, to muse and to rove, which gave these *Kotogakko* friendships their distinctive character. Everything else in the life of a Japanese might depend on circumstances; the *Kotogakko* mateship was absolute.

Similar phenomena of less strength and depth were observed in other quarters. If an officer was appointed to a high post the papers would invariably mention the graduation year class to which he belonged while in the Military Academy; and the press would name those who had graduated at the same time. In the universities such traits were much less in evidence; the student entered the university at a rather late age, compared with the student in the West, and his decisive friendships had already been formed at the *Kotogakko*. This may be one of the foremost reasons why the universities played a comparatively small part in the formation of the Japanese. The mind of the Japanese university student had already been set. What he sought in the university seems to have been not inspiration and self-development, but the acquisition of knowledge and abilities useful for his career. He was often married, and almost invariably preoccupied with the problem of how to earn a living in the near future. Separated from his *Kotogakko* mate he remained as a rule a solitary figure, talking only to students who had graduated from his School, considering the university mainly as a machine for smooth graduating and swift job-getting

PATRON AND CLIENT

Among the social ties binding together unequals the patron-client relation was, and is likely to remain, in Japan by far the most important, all-pervading, of remarkable stability, and often of overriding strength. The Japanese is quick to observe differences in personal power, pull, dependability and prestige; and he will put his service and assent at the disposal of a potential patron often in forms verging on abject flattery and disregard of dignity. Everybody is by turns patron and client, the Minister of State, the geisha, the official, the teacher, the maid; not only *de facto* and almost unconsciously, as in Western society, but also *quasi de jure* and in perfect lucidity, patronising people below, serving people above, one's place on the ladder of social existence. If one wishes to know what a man is capable of doing or of leaving undone, it is not enough to know his legal status and his professional record, his capital resources and his family: it may be of greater consequence to know who his patron is and on which clients he can count. Such relations exist in every society, in more or less veiled grades of strength and legitimacy. In Japan not only are they more numerous, but they also constitute one of the two central archetypes of social organisation. What is often called "feudalism" (a rather promiscuous term unfit to serve sociological analysis unless strictly defined) is in fact a network of patron-client relations, a much older and more universal type of social obligation carrying with it the sanction proper to unwritten laws: to break these bonds without sufficient reason would make the offender an "impossible" man.

In some respects, though not legally, the Japanese patron–client relationship recalls the ancient Roman bond from which I have borrowed these terms. To fail his clients was in antiquity deemed one of the greatest offences a Roman citizen could perpetrate. Every morning, at a very early hour, a Roman man of rank and influence would receive the swarm of his clients and hear their requests before he resumed his daily routine. Japanese of similar status seem to begin their working day in a similar fashion. Many attitudes and affairs are settled in these parleys shortly after sunrise, in an atmosphere of informality, but near the shelf where the house-gods are living.

In times of need the nexus will become visible. If, for example, a house is on fire, all those indebted for some reason to the proprietor will arrive in haste in order to be of help and comfort. If a man is unable to help his client against powerful adversaries or political currents he has lost face and hides his shame in awkward silence.

THE FAMILY

The importance of the age group and of the patron-client relationship is in inverse proportion to the frequency with which they are mentioned. The role played by the "family system" in Japanese society is much talked of and written about; but the actual significance of ties of consanguinity has often been overestimated. In its present form at least, the so-called family system is a late growth, deliberately transplanted from China and rigidly rationalised for the political ends of the Tokugawa Shogunate. Early Japanese literature knows comparatively little of these obligations and of the corresponding "ancestor-cult" which seems to be at variance with the native attitudes towards the dead. The very rigidity of these rules and rites, contrasting sharply with the fluidity and suppleness peculiar to Japanese ways of life, points to a foreign origin and purposive exploitation.

The small family unit, organised strictly on the principle of primogeniture and masculine superiority, crystallised in the centuries of civil war preceding the Tokugawa era. Under the rule of the Neo-Confucian state-philosophers who advised the Shogun it was made into a cellular model of patriarchal autocracy, strict subordination balanced by benevolence and justice. Buddhist forms of the care for the dead and Chinese theories of "filial piety" were utilised to hedge in the relations of parents and children with a formal and unchangeable framework of rites and customs. The natural ties of affection binding the members of a small family have always been strong with the Japanese, a highly emotional race. What is called the "family system" is less a result of such feelings than a political structure in miniature, with roots reaching far back into the times of gentilitial organisation.

Even after this "system" became subject to the corrosive forces of modern economic life and urban individualisation, the Japanese family continued to resemble a small authoritarian state. Its constitution was strictly monarchical, and property was transferred in its entirety to the son (not necessarily the eldest) who succeeded the paterfamilias, either upon the latter's death or on his voluntary retirement as *inkyo*. The head of the family acted after having consulted the family council, which closely resembled a tribal Council of Elders.

The "political" character of the Japanese family was shown also by the frequency of adoption of sons. The function of this practice was not always, as in China, to provide for a male heir able to perform the rites of ancestor-worship. Often a second son was adopted if the physical son was thought to be more lazy, or less talented, than the adopted boy. Physical consanguinity by male line has played, therefore, a smaller part in family history in Japan than in the modern West. It is for this reason perhaps that Japanese houses of considerable antiquity have retained their vitality.

THE NATION-FAMILY MYTH

Only because the Japanese family was an empire *in nucleo* was it possible to conceive of the empire as a great family, thus conferring on the large society the advantageous characteristics of a small group.

From the standpoint of historical truth, it is difficult to understand how the whole Japanese nation could be called a family of families ruled over by the *Tenno* (Emperor) as head of the germinal clan from which all other families are derived. Modern anthropological research has not yet solved the problem of the racial composition of the Japanese, but it leaves no doubt that they are the product of intermarriage of very different racial strains which are also found in other parts of Asia and in Europe. The official mythologies of ancient Japan distinguish clearly and without embarrassment between different strands of blood, even in the ruling class of archaic ages. The difference between the descendants of Amaterasu-o-mikami, the sun goddess, and of other deities, called "earthy", is absolute. Moreover, genealogical tables compiled in the ninth century A.D. show that one third of the aristocracy claimed Chinese or Korean descent.

A remarkable number of persons, it is true, might well be able to trace descent from an Imperial prince either by legitimate or by illegitimate unions with the daughters of aristocrats or commoners; but the claim of all Japanese to be descended from Amaterasu-o-mikami as their first ancestor should have been regarded as sacrilegious from the viewpoint of Shinto traditions. Apparently, we are confronted here with a "prelogical" idea characteristic of primitive thought, with its stubborn impermeability to the demand for logical coherence and evidence. The strangest fact is that this quasi-myth emerged only quite recently, in an era of intensive Westernisation of intellectual processes and social conditions. It is as different from the original ancestor myths of the *Kojiki* and *Nihongi* as the mythical lore of ancient Greece was from the Gnostic doctrines or other Hellenistic creeds.★

The readiness of modern Japanese to embrace this irrational belief, which seemed to serve certain political tendencies very well although it ran counter to venerable traditions, must have been greatly facilitated by the political structure of a Japanese family.

The organic function of this quasi-myth is unmistakable. It nourished in a society exposed to a host of disintegrating influences, acting from within and from abroad, the precious feeling that all Japanese were brothers and the conviction that they might look up to their ruler as to a father. Even the poorest and weakest member of the nation was made to believe that in some undefined way he was the bearer of the mysterious forces transmitted by the sun goddess to her posterity.

The spirit of the small group never demonstrated its power, to

★ The *Nihongi* (or *Nihon-shoki*), a collection of ancient chronicles, was compiled in thirty volumes in 720 A.D. With the *Kojiki* (see footnote on page 44), it is the oldest authority for the primitive period of Japanese history. [Ed.]

bind and preserve, more clearly than at the time when the defeated Japanese rallied to their monarch as the pillar of their very existence—despite the fact that before the war he had endorsed the fatefully wrong decisions of his advisers and, after the war, had denied his special divinity in the New Year Rescript of 1946. The myth of imperial "divinity" had served to form a self-supporting pattern of emotions and attitudes of such structural strength that it could now be declared to be a mere symbol. It has probably never been taken literally except by half-witted fanatics and by half-learned foreigners.

NOTES

1 Yukio Ozaki, *The Voice of Japanese Democracy*, Yokohama, 1918, p. 90 *et seq.*
2 Sobei Mogi and H. Vere Redman, *The Problem of the Far East*, London, 1935, p. 126.
3 J. Murdoch and I. Yamagata, *A History of Japan*, London, 1925, p. 416.
4 K. Asakawa, *Documents of Iriki*, New Haven, Yale, 1928, pp. 295–6, 239–41.
5 John F. Embree, *Suye Mura*, Chicago, 1939, p. 87.

6

The Geometry of Japanese Culture

THE PATTERN OF PATTERNS

A stranger landing on the islands of Japan will soon perceive that he has entered a world that follows a law of its own in every province of action and contemplation; a field of strange and strong magnetic forces; a social and mental space ruled by an unaccustomed geometry. Centre of gravitation and lines of least resistance are determined in unfamiliar ways; rivers are running in unpredictable rhythms towards unknown seas; the sense of orientation and the scales of preference are subtly disturbed by a general "topsy-turvydom" expressing itself in almost systematic exchanges of left and right, before and after, speech and silence. Every gesture, the shape of vessels, the cadence of a sentence, the etiquette of a household or of a school-class, an arrangement of flowers in a vase—each bears an unmistakable mark peculiar to just this country.

Not that all things we meet in this sphere were mechanically modelled upon the same pattern: there is obviously a great breadth of variability and autonomy within the general framework; and the more intimately this system is known the more it appears not as an order imposed from without and above, but as a *Gestaltung*, a coordinated whole of activities and attitudes able to support itself and restore its order against disturbances from within or without; a *Gestaltung* moulded and remoulded in a process in which the patterns governing each field are woven into a pattern of a higher order, of greater integrative range and force.

This "pattern of patterns" regulates the relations of man to man, of public life to private existence, of art and philosophy, politics and mythology, erotics and law, and provides all elements of a given culture with a kind of family resemblance, which cannot be derived by deduction from a conceptual principle nor achieved by rational planning but follows from the peculiar way in which all parts are interacting. Within this self-generating structure—an ever-changing, growing and decaying, nexus of acts and attitudes—nobody is free "to do as he likes" (provided he does not undertake to live outside its pale, as a hermit, a courtesan, a tramp—and even for these there is a conventionally unorthodox way of life outlined for them by the pattern of patterns); yet the whole of this microcosm lives on, through serene and agitated periods, with a degree of coordination, adaptation and logic of growth commonly held to be peculiar to the organisms of plant and animal life.

It is this character of a society which defines its civilisation or, following German usage, its culture. It would be awkward to reserve this term either for states achieving a certain measure of tolerance, politeness, rationality and sympathy—which are indeed common features of very different civilisations in certain phases of their life—or to accumulations of intellectual and aesthetic achievements and enjoyments, as contrasted with the ordinary humdrum life of a society—a conception peculiar to certain late stages of different cultures, where production and appreciation of works of art and science tend to be split off from the common work and striving of a group. In both cases particular traits shared by several civilisations in specific situations are identified with the essence of culture.

A more catholic definition is needed if different types of culture are to be compared, their individualities characterised, their significance and their limitations interpreted. The basic phenomenon is not the diminution of suffering and violence, nor the emergence of painting, metaphysics, and lectures thereon, but the formation of what we have called a pattern of patterns resembling the unity of a personality that has achieved *Ganzheit,* wholeness.

It aspires towards unity of style in the works of an author or in a school of art, and it partakes of the fundamental gift of life: to create self-sustaining structures able to endure; to grow and to procreate.

It is the presence of such a structure, or, more precisely, *Gestaltung,* which is felt by the foreigner in his first contacts with a new social and mental environment, in various degrees corresponding to his own sensitivity and penetration, but also to the measure in which the foreign civilisation has proved her integrative power. The spectator is free, if he should be a strict nominalist, to deny in his ontological reasoning the existence of such structures; however, he will have to acknowledge their awkward or attractive "suchness" and specific energy in every phase of his daily life. If he fails to do so he is liable to find himself soon enmeshed in a maze of unconnected experiences, mostly of an unpleasant nature; and for their interpretation he finds himself relying only on vague analogies and treacherous *quid pro quos,* surrogate forms of genuine unity in diversity . . .

> "Holding all the parts in his hand,
> Lacking alas! the inner bond."
>
> *"Dann hat er die Teile in seiner Hand,*
> *Fehlt, leider! nur das geistige Band."*
> (Goethe)

SEQUENCES AND LAWS

The unwritten norm of a civilisation resembles a melody more than what modern physicists and jurists call a law. It is an historical growth, never identical with—nor exhausted by—any cross-section made at a certain date, even if it be the culminating point of that culture. A civilisation is a fabric that extends its sway not only in space but also in time; its present cannot be understood without constant reference to its roots in the past and to its anticipations of the future. Certain products of a civilisation, poems and rituals, philosophies and technologies, may claim some kind of universal validity, in relative freedom from the limitations of space and time; but they cannot be understood if they are not first seen as children of a specific soil, of a determinate hour of history. They gain significance for other civilisations only on condition of having first served their mother civilisation, in a unique situation in which a man-creator became the founder of a spiritual race by answering a riddle of the sphinx or a voice from a burning bush. The fundamental distinction is not between societies of different ideas and aims, but between those awake at the hour of spiritual destiny, able to find their own word in answer to the call and to sustain and guard the life of this word, and those that have failed. The infant societies we call primitive have not yet found such a word. Those lingering on in stereotyped ways after the word had exhausted its inner force may be called reverberative; to this type belong the Egyptian civilisation after the end of the Ramessides, Chinese civilisation after the Han dynasty, and Indian civilisation after King Asoka.

Finding a new Word and keeping it alive in ever-changing forms is the work of the spirit and therefore unpredictable. A civilisation, however, is the process in which the spirit compels and persuades matter to carry its imprint in the shape of enduring configurations (*Gestalten, Gestaltungen*), and as this matter—the basic structure of man, his mind, and his geographical environment—is largely homogenous, it may be expected that the emergence, transformation, and decay of such patterns should follow laws comparable with those ruling other organic units.

Every mature civilisation conceives of itself in terms of a personality, thinking back to its childhood; dwelling on its ripening into manhood; fixing a culminating point, the "great noon" of its life; learning, reluctantly, to know when the full development of its potentialities marks the beginning of descent, when growing clarity and power must be purchased with lessening creative powers; finally deciding, after a period of intensified strife and mental agony, to desire nothing better than stability, quiet, order and content, while it surrenders to others the Promethean task of subduing chaos into new form.

Within the framework created by such final structures, of which the *Imperium Romanum* after Augustus, the Han Empire of the Chinese, and the New Empire of Egypt, are the great examples, a reverberating civilisation may uphold the life of precious traditions, mixed in varying proportions with new cultural elements and in a synchretistic way. It may continue to produce rare men of genius and choice works of art, but all this will be of the nature of episodes more or less brief, more or less disconnected. The true life of a classic civilisation is lived between a sacral archaic kingdom and a late sceptical empire. It is bound up with the fate of a body politic which follows the same law in its own field as religion, art, poetry, knowledge and other provinces of human life. Before and after such a body politic has won the power of self-sustained duration there may be much talent, vigour, and interest; but there cannot be that organic unit which constitutes the essence of civilisation. The idea of an unpolitical civilisation is the day-dream of a society that has lost its bearings.

It is not suggested that all civilisations must strictly follow the pattern indicated, nor that the course of their history can be predicted. The pattern represents an "ideal type", a conceptual model serving to demonstrate the genetic law of a classic society. Japanese civilisation belongs to this class of mature societies.

THE JAPANESE EXAMPLE

It is one of the most characteristic traits of Japanese life that it has reduced the realm of genius to a bare minimum, with a rigour unknown in any other great civilisation. There are fewer creative personalities, to each of these a smaller amplitude of being different is conceded. With a unique determination and persistence, stress is laid on the harmony of the whole, on unbroken continuity, on jealous safeguarding of enduring patterns which are preferably enshrined in semi-conscious automatisms. These qualities, while perhaps hindering Japanese civilisation from producing many men or many works of more than national significance, have helped to give the whole of Japanese civilisation a paradigmatic value.

Japan has to offer few contributions to world culture except this signal one: to have given an example of a style of life subordinating everything to one value: duration.

The first signs of a civilisation that can be recognised as genuinely Japanese emerge in the course of the third century A.D., under the half-historical reign of Sujin *Tenno*. The new civilisation grows into its first spring during the Asuka, Nara, and early Heian periods, from the sixth century to the end of the ninth; it rises to its zenith in the later Heian (Fujiwara) age (tenth century to the twelfth) and in the Kamakura period (twelfth century to the fourteenth)—epochs divided by the appearance of religious reformers both individualistic and nation-bound. After a Time of Troubles (to use Toynbee's terminology), harbouring an exquisite aesthetic culture in which the canons of Japanese taste and behaviour are defined, the civilisation reaches its final stage, politically static-minded and culturally fully democratised, under the Tokugawa (seventeenth century to the middle of the nineteenth), a condition modified only superficially by the reception of Western elements of civilisation after 1868.

The succession of cultural phases recalls in many significant details a similar rhythm in Western and Central European civilisation, whose evolution seems to follow with a time lag of two to three centuries but which represents throughout its course a "later" phase of cultural history than Japan. The latter, owing to her Oriental character, prefers to rest on tradition, custom, communal life, while the West has dared to shoot its arrows further in the direction of individuality, *ratio*, and freedom.

However, it would be a mistake of considerable magnitude to classify Japanese civilisation for this reason as rudimentary. In seeking the essentials of a civilisation it is all-important not to be misled by easy analogies into missing the true "synchronisms". The rise of town life, for example, occurs later in Japan than in the West; so does the emergence of scientific research, of widespread mercantile enterprise, or rationalised technology. But it must not be forgotten that these values play, by virtue of the pattern of Japanese culture, another role in Japan than in England or Germany; no genuine Japanese could have thought of conceiving of history as "progress in the realisation of freedom", or of calling man a tool-making animal.

What corresponds in Japanese cultural history to the epoch of the many classical city-states, or the many medieval and early Renaissance towns, is the Heian era, in which the whole life of the nation is concentrated in the one capital; its norms are given shape not in the intercourse and rivalry of confederated clans or guilds as in Athens or Genoa, London or Cologne, but within the court society swayed by the one Fujiwara clan, the breeding group of Imperial mothers and concubines. It is here that Japanese life first realises itself in autochthonous forms that have made life itself an art, poetry a cult, ceremony a living force. Later ages have produced poems and theologies more subtle or more bold, more delicately shaded, or more abruptly profound; but in the writings of Murasaki Shikibu and Sei Shonagon, in the *emaki-mono* illustrating their works, in the few remnants of Fujiwara architecture, there is a wholeness, balance, poise and reserve attainable only in those earliest hours of a society's glow when the dew of the morning is still on the leaves, and beauty has not yet begun to die from its own perfection.

It is significant that Japan's two greatest writers, and some of her best poets, have been women. The Japanese mind, leaning towards unadulterated emotion, unconscious gliding, subtle observation and sudden turns, is bound to favour female ways of self-expression on the higher planes of cultural life. Nor can it be pure chance that their chief deity has assumed a female character. It is only in the later stages of Japanese culture that women disappear more and more into the private background of the home and of the tea-house "societies of willows and flowers". The masculine element asserts itself first in the great achievement of the Kamakura age (which seems to correspond "synchronically" to the sixteenth and seventeenth centuries in the West): namely, the erection of a secular political framework of unified administration and military efficiency; to be solidified finally, after centuries of rivalry and internal war, into the Tokugawa Shogunate. In the history of the West the descending branch of the parabola of culture seems to exhibit increasingly female characteristics; the corresponding phases of Japanese civilisation witness a recrudescence of masculine qualities. The dualism between the feminine-minded bearers of culture and the masculine-minded personalities who built and preserved the State has never been more pronounced than in the Meiji Revolution, which was carried through by ultra-virile warrior-*samurai* of low rank, to most of whom literature and art meant nothing.

DOMINANT QUALITIES

Few things are more futile than attempts to define the nature of a nation, a civilisation, a personality, by pointing to a single quality: courage or gracefulness, profundity or arrogance, form or freedom. What constitutes the character of a living being is a pattern of movement, or rather of movement of movements. The nature of such patterns defies description by a single term but may be understood as the solution of a problem, the mastering of a task, that a particular form of life has set itself. A first approximation may be gained by naming at least two contrasting qualities, the blending of which has here been achieved: thus the German mind combines the will to widest universality with the sense for the most individual; the Italian mind combines enthusiastic ardour with pellucid rationality; the French, the spirit of geometry with the spirit of subtlety; the English, striving for personal liberty with readiness to submit to social convention.

The Japanese mind and its products, at their best, bear the mark of two qualities rarely, if ever, united in one civilisation: nearness to origins (*Ursprünglichkeit*) and aristocratic distinction (*Vornehmheit*). The first trait is shared, for example, by Russia; the second, by France. The blending of both gives Japanese works of art and forms of life a quality of refinement that appears not as a result of a long process of sublimation, but as a spontaneous gift of nature. Foreshadowed in the archaic poetry of the Nara age and attaining mellowness in the style of the Ashikaga period, this quality has found, not accidentally, its classical expression in the works of the two great women writers of the Heian age. For it is most natural for women to display rare achievements as if they were born without strife, and to produce the exquisite and fastidious without leaving the sphere where life springs up and ever renews itself.

RELATION TO FOREIGN CULTURES

Another distinctly feminine trait of Japanese culture may be found in its readiness to yield to foreign influences, sometimes carried to such extremes that its own nature seems to be driven underground for very long periods. Nietzsche distinguished between two archetypes of men of genius and of civilisations: one virile, procreative, establishing new forms of life and scales of values; the other feminine, waiting to be made fecund, devoted to the work of bearing, nursing, completing. It is doubtful whether this classification is as trenchant as it looks. The Greeks, classified as feminine by Nietzsche, seem to partake of both characteristics in equal degree. As for the Japanese, their place in this scheme is not uncertain. They invent few things, receive passionately, and excel in the art of adapting, adjusting, fitting. They are exceptionally shrewd in sifting and excluding. What they have chosen to undertake is often reduced in scale or scope but within these limits is carried to perfection.

The way in which the Japanese proceed in assimilating foreign elements of culture—ideas, styles, institutions, creeds—often resembles somewhat the mimicry of animals, or the submission by women to a new fashion. Models are selected and scrupulously copied in every detail. What attracts their attention is always the new, the contemporary, the modern. There are few instances of an urge to evoke the spirit of another age, however great. Even after three generations of intensive and extensive Westernisation the central works and ideas of Mediterranean classical antiquity, of the Western and Central European Middle Ages, or even of their Renaissance, have not yet become a living force; such knowledge as has been sought is restricted to a small circle or specialist scholars; there are very few traces of a personal interest in the sources of European greatness. Of contemporary writers every satellite from the second order downwards is assiduously read and utilised.

It was not altogether different in the age of the first reception of Chinese civilisation, although the ostensible continuity or Chinese philosophy and poetry, art and political doctrine, may have contributed to veil this phenomenon. In his jealous communion with himself the Japanese knows very well the desire to evoke the past by going back to the origin, the "true source", in which things and men were still unadulterated and genuine. From foreign countries no such regenerating impulses are expected. The leading motive is to be up-to-date, not to fall behind what others have achieved, to know the watchword of the hour. It thus happens that alien elements taken over without their roots are robbed of their procreative power and soon become conventionalised.

It is easy to enumerate what has been acquired in these assimilative processes during the last fifteen hundred years: from (or through) China, ceremonial and music, Confucian classics and Taoist wisdom, Buddhist speculations and Tantric mysteries, the style of Sung painting and the writing of Chinese verse, calendar making and mantic arts; from Europe, technology and administration, medicine and natural philosophy, dress and food, political strife and business routine, critical thought and analytical literature.[1] It is no less important to realise what has not been found acceptable: the monumental art of China's archaic bronze vessels, the monochrome ceramics of the Ch'ing period, the philosophy of the "Legalist School", the rhapsodies of the Han period; the whole world of Greece and Rome, the poetry and painting of the European Renaissance, of Rembrandt and Rubens; the work of the deepest European thinkers and the spirit of the great European historians. The list is by no means complete.

The guiding principles of selection have been in most cases utilitarian and political. Throughout their history the Japanese have shown a preference for what promised greater power and prestige for the nation, and for what appealed to the curiosity and appetite for novelties of the individual; they have tended to eliminate everything, however great, if it was felt to threaten the continuity of Japanese life, to imperil the stability of their political structure, and to alienate the individual from his congenital group. There is a perfect logic of an organic nature in these processes of assimilation and exclusion. One may wish the Japanese were different; but one cannot hold that they are imitators. Few civilisations have been in essence more autochthonous.

It is not only in its principle of selection that the autonomous moulding power of Japanese culture has manifested itself. Every element entering this sphere is by virtue of a secret alchemy changed into something neither intended nor appreciated by its originators abroad. The outer form of Western civil administration, higher education, fighting services, church and journalism may have been borrowed: their ways of functioning differ profoundly from their Western counterparts. A Chinese of the T'ang or Sung periods may not have felt less bewildered if it had fallen to his lot to observe Chinese ceremonial, art and scholarship shortly after their introduction to Japan, growing there into an exotic plant different in all but externals, and serving alien purposes. The most drastic proof of the existence of a specific Japanese civilisation is perhaps the impossibility for any typical Chinese or Westerniser to live in this medium without feeling slightly oppressed even when charmed, subtly excluded even if allowed to participate. Moments of perfect congruence may occur, but they are rare and fugitive.

If it is argued that the proportion of what has been introduced from abroad and what is home-grown indicates a rather low degree of Japanese productivity, it is only fair to remember what Western and Central European civilisation owes to Egypt, Babylon, Palestine, Greece, Rome, Persia and India; what Renaissance Italy and France, in her grand century, have given to England and Germany; and what exchanges the countries of

Shakespeare and Goethe have made. Japanese civilisation is characterised less by its foreign indebtedness than by the relative insignificance of Japan's past contributions to the cultural life of other nations.

LACK OF EMISSIVE POWER

Japan's most distinctive creations have no foreign model. Neither Murasaki Shikibu's novel nor the *No*-plays, neither the *uta* nor the *haiku* poems, the *Yamato-e* or the *Ukiyo-e* school of painting and drawing, have Chinese antecedents; and the one incomparable writer of the Meiji period, Higuchi Ichiyo, follows the Murasaki tradition rather than Western currents. These facts appear to have remained unknown to the Western public and its journalistic guides, because until quite recently Japanese literary works have been translated or made accessible only in inadequate versions. And it was difficult indeed to gain an intimate knowledge of Japanese painting from European museums and collections. But the problem remains why this gifted and active nation has produced so little that has been found acceptable by other countries in an age open to all foreign influences. Contact with Japanese fine arts has refreshed the European sense of colour and bold design and has confirmed intrepid architects in their heterodox trends; a first acquaintance with Japanese poetry may have conveyed to some Western writers a touch of lightness and birdlike grace. Our ceramics have profited considerably, as have the principles of our domestic interior decoration. Is this all a nation that aspired to be the leading power of East Asia, and beyond, can give? Japanese scientists have made considerable contributions to the common fund of mathematics and medicine. No philosopher able to command much attention abroad has arisen. Where is the word of oecumenical validity that Japan has found which would justify her claim to greatness?

Before an attempt can be made to answer this crucial question, two observations may be advanced. It is doubtful whether the value of a specific civilisation depends on what can be generalised and can serve as a pattern to foreign civilisations. Dante has wielded less influence abroad than Petrarca who is second in rank to him; Heine has conquered a European public much larger and more grateful than that actually ruled by Goethe; Chopin was more widely received than Bach. As in the sphere of industrial production and marketing, the products exported are not always those appreciated most in the home market. Even the fame of André Gide, of George Bernard Shaw, of Dostoievsky, was for a long time, and may continue to be, disproportionately greater among foreign readers than among their countrymen. The best a race produces is likely to be so specialised, expressive of its inmost needs and possibilities, or so vast and profound, and thus inaccessible to the common reader, that it will reach a foreign public only in those rare cases where genius recognises genius, and translators and interpreters of quite unusual gifts can mediate. The existence of a poet of the order of magnitude of the Dane, Jens Peter Jacobsen, or of the Dutch Albert Verwey, seems to be still largely unknown in England or France. It may well be that the choicest Japan had to offer has not been able to find international fame not because it lacks creative force, but because it bears too strongly the stamp of the race that has produced it.

Moreover, an exchange of cultural elements is a two-sided affair: it needs not only a party able to give, but also a party ready to receive; and this readiness is often not a matter of free will and generally receptive dispositions but is conditioned by the specific phase a civilisation is living through: in a culture that has not lost its instincts altogether not everything desirable will be found acceptable at every hour. The philosophy of Chu Hsi (twelfth century A.D.) had to wait five hundred years for its reception in Japan under the Tokugawa Shogunate. Shakespeare did not become a living force in Germany until the youth of Goethe.

The wood-cuts and the ceramics of Japan were introduced in Europe at a propitious moment, when the arts began to emancipate themselves from classical canons and naturalist preoccupations, thus becoming free to receive a new message of flowing motion and detached lightness, delicacy of colour and audacity of line. But these qualities also limited the influence of Japanese art to what suited the impressionist and decorative tendencies of the receiving countries at that moment. The spirit of classical Japanese painting, and of Japanese poetry too, is still in the first stages of penetrating the consciousness of the West.

LIMITS AND ACHIEVEMENTS

The fundamental cause of Japan's apparent lack of cultural emissive power, I find, however, in the true character of her achievements: the slow, organic growth of a civilisation combining endurance and plasticity; highly aristocratic and yet capable of permeating all classes of a strongly stratified society: a complex and indivisible whole, nursing the life of its members with its peculiar spirit. These achievements have been bought at the price of hindering (though not quite preventing) the emergence of great solitary figures of genius far in advance of their age and society and, not less, the crystallisation of those self-sufficing structures of thought, of law, of artistic creation, in which the genius of Europe has excelled.

In Japan the spirit seems reluctant to leave the sphere of common life: it remains anxious to realise not the maximum of *creation* but of *duration,* of social coherence and homogeneity, not of individual strength and tension. There is no Japanese equivalent to the *Oresteia;* no *Timaios,* no *Divina Comedia,* no *Sistina,* no *Hamlet* and no *Faust,* no *Matthaeus Passion* and no *Fleurs du Mal.* But whatever the Japanese have produced has entered the life of the ordinary man with a flexibility and omnipresence unknown in the West, saturating it, as it were, with fine particles of grace and light. Society has been woven into a fabric that resembles a work of art without losing the character of a natural growth closely communing with the maternal forces of Nature. It is in this sense that Japanese civilisation, while remaining inimitable in detail, can be called a model, if taken as a whole. It describes a circle of smaller radius than that of Europe, but it has known how to close it.

The philosopher Georg Simmel saw the decisive trait of "the tragedy of modern culture" in the wide disparity between the beauty and greatness of its objective attainments, in the shape of works of art, systems of law, metaphysical constructions, which tend more and more to live a life of their own, and the growing shapelessness and jejuneness of ordinary human existence. For the Japanese, in so far as they are still moulded by their autochthonous culture, this disparity does not exist. Their ways cannot become ours, but they show, as in a reducing mirror, the nature of a civilisation that has achieved integration.

NOTES

1 Izuru Shimura, *Western Influences on Japanese History and Culture in Earlier Periods (1540–1860)*, Tokyo, 1936.

7

The Contrasts of Japan and China

POLARISATION

It is not only as givers and receivers of elements of culture that civilisations act upon each other. A more obscure but not less significant relation is established by impacts that produce a process of polarisation: forces of one society calling forth opposite forces in the other. In some cases such an antithetical movement is due to the presence of conscious opposition, antagonistic urges, enjoyment of contradiction. More often it is caused by half-conscious or unconscious tendencies through which the organic dialectics of life appear to work themselves out. Thus Greek and Roman classical art and literature served not only as model and standard for West European civilisation but also as thesis engendering an antithesis, inducing a shift of emphasis from order to freedom, from generality to individuality, from the body to the spirit. Contact with French society has sometimes added touches of lightness and grace to German literature; but it has also reinforced the appreciation of what is massive, systematic, unsociable and primordial. Similarly China has perhaps rendered the most signal service to Japan, by awakening the Japanese mind to its own contrasting potentialities. It is by transforming the impulses received from China into means of discovering herself that Japan has vindicated her claim as a culture able to live according to its own law. The presence of this law can be perceived in every sphere of life, from simple gesture to metaphysical construction.

SYMBOLIC ATTITUDES

If, closing the eyes, one tries to conjure up the figures of a typical
Chinese (preferably from the north, where Chinese civilisation was
created) and a typical Japanese in their most significant attitudes,
there appears first a man erect, solid and well poised, looking at
the world with a steady quiet gaze and standing in clear outline
against an invariable sky; then there emerges the swift adroit
movement of an unimposing being from a variegated background
of irregular forms, opalescent veils, and almost imperceptible
scents. The gestures of a well-mannered Chinese are round,
dignified, even ponderous: our memory retains of them not the
act of movement but a sequence of impressive postures. The
Japanese too, if trained in classical etiquette, knows how to rest
in a graceful and austere manner: but even his states of repose
seem to prefigure and prepare a nascent movement.

These contrasts are not the product of mere differences of
aesthetic sensibility; they point to more deep-seated polarities.
In the movements of the Chinese a substance expresses the laws
of its structure. The movements of a Japanese seem not to originate
in his frail body but to avail themselves of it, charging it with a
current of demonic power, or of mysterious grace, making him
bend and bow and vibrate like a tree in wind and rain. A Chinese
when pointing at an object makes a firm imperative gesture
which builds into space a solid system of co-ordinates. The
Japanese sketches a slight swift, indicative, gesture, just sufficient
to lead the eye and change thereby the direction of some latent
forces.

COSMIC ORDER

A traveller arriving in North China after spending years in the
Japanese islands, observing for the first time those compact figures
and that imperturbable gaze of men standing along the railway
embankments, feels tempted to ask himself whether he ever saw
in Japan persons in an upright position, as if lost in the act of
disinterested beholding. In that Chinese attitude there seems to

survive a trace of the pathos of the first man who dared to stand erect, and who awoke to *see*. No longer enmeshed in that closed, instinct-bound circuit of desires and satisfactions, impulses and signals for action in which we suppose the animal to move, leaving the sheltering and fearsome chaos of the primeval forest where everything seems to melt into everything in a hopeless tangle, he has suddenly gained the freedom of perceiving and thinking true objects, "*Gegenstände*"—persevering entities, endowed with a power to exist independently of him, and yet obeying the same dimly foreshadowed laws and rhythms to which his own existence remains subject.

Around him as a centre an endless plain is spreading, orientated in the form of a cross created by the natural co-ordinates of right and left, before and behind. These directions radiate from the very point where he is standing; correspondingly, the axis of his own erect body points above him to the centre of the sky. He takes this system of orientation with him wherever he goes. Later he may learn to give it a new definiteness and generality by observing the regular motions of the sun and of other stars; he will increase his awareness of a cosmic symmetry and order, whether immanent in this world or emanating from a transcendent will, or more probably partaking of both. Right and left, above and below, light and darkness will come to designate phases and stations of regular and recurrent changes, day and night, the months and the seasons, and, much later, cosmic cycles. The great scales of the universe, in this primordial cosmic view, always carry equal weights; they may be called by many names, designated by many emblems: male and female, heaven and earth, ruler and people, victory and defeat. This world is throughout symmetrically structured, like space itself, and its Way (*tao*) and Power (*te*) are the alternating play of elements, aspects, patterns. Of these, five is the natural number, for they correspond to the five original cardinal points of space, the fifth being the centre of the cosmic square that survives in the shape of Chinese jade-symbols of the Earth or the apex of a pyramid. Each of these elements partakes both of changing fate and of rhythmic permanence, each defeating its predecessor in a sequence determined by cosmic rhythm, devouring the vanquished and being devoured in turn, but always in such a way as to leave a small remainder which may grow and inaugurate a new cycle.

These are well-known fundamental concepts of early Chinese cosmology. The quietly gazing men on the embankments may never have heard of the metaphysical legacies of the classical age of their race, except in dim echoes of folklore, but their attitudes and moods seem to be made out of the same substance that gave birth to the cosmological speculations and classifications of the thinkers and scholars of Ancient China, and from which those thoughts drew their vitality: there is no abstract idea which has not been distilled from the sap of individual men and women.

THE DEED

The eye of the Japanese is not lost in the vision of celestial-telluric harmonies. It is quick to observe just those signals from the outer world that concern his life or that of his clan. It likes to withdraw from that outward sphere and to rest attentively behind closed lids, or in a stare that appears to recognize no external object. The regard of the Japanese seems to be a kind of tense listening . . . waiting for the sound that calls for action. There are so many voices and rustlings around him (the primeval forest with its unseen dangers seems to haunt him for ever), and he has to notice them all, but he argues with none. If the moment for making a decision has come, all this tumult, he knows, will subside abruptly, and out of the tense silence there will emerge with inexorable swiftness and force the deed that asks to be done by him—as a sword that, as in Japanese hero-tales, carries forward the arm of the warrior rather than being wielded by him.

The Japanese gaze can dwell admiringly, lovingly, ecstatically, on a short-lived flower, a storm-tortured tree trunk, a god-like towering peak; but these are to him not objects of a vision which finds repose in the contemplation of beauty and order. They too are signs and carry a message to his soul, calling him back to himself, or asking him to transcend himself, admonishing him to exchange space-bound reality and personal existence for a mode of being that carries him beyond the confines of life and death.

THE SELF

If there is a law governing this un-cosmic world of the Japanese, both in his highest modes of being where he aims at the Absolute and in his everyday life where he is concerned with mere utilities, it can only be a law of inescapable change and universal impermanence. In no literature of a great nation is there less room than here for the pure radiance of the stars and for the geometrical order of their courses; neither the Pythagorean harmony of the spheres nor the Platonic idea of ideas speaks to the Japanese. Identity, Measure, Immutability do not correspond to inborn needs of his soul. The Absolute itself becomes a process, Annihilation rather than The Nought. World, to him, is not a comprehensive whole, but the locus of withdrawals into his Self. For everything leads the Japanese back to himself; to him seeing is a circuit. His is the existence of a Monad leading a life that gravitates on an internal abyss of whirlpool-like forces. Either this self is defined by his group, his family, or the family of families which is the Japanese nation, centred on the Imperial Ruler, *Tenno*, who is himself nothing but a Medium, mediating between his ancestor gods on high and his subjects, not a figure in his own right. Or the Self is found in the Buddha nature of things and beings, the annihilation of their individual existence, a process of transcending rather than anything transcendent. In both cases, reaching the Self, realising the Way, means sacrifice; unconditional and often frantic self-abandonment seeking "the shortest path back into the All" (Hoelderlin: "*ins All zurück die kürzeste Bahn*").

In his everyday existence the Japanese acts, feels, thinks, decides, as if Japan would act through him; if asked to what extent his acts emanate from himself, and to what extent from his group, he would not only be unable to give a rational account but he would also be unwilling to admit the validity of the question. He stands to his group in a relation in which we imagine the life of a cell stands to the life of an organism; or, at the very least, it approximates to that relation in a degree observable in no other civilised nation. If the Japanese wants to sever these congenital bonds, there is no choice left for him but to destroy all ties of birth and allegiance, withdrawing not only from his group but also from the whole world of impermanence, entering the Buddhist path which promises to lead to the complete annihilation of "this fleeting world".

DELIVERANCE

It has been a puzzle to many observers that Japan, intensely nationalist, military-minded, self-centred, has become the one great nation that has adhered to Buddhism, a religion discarded in India, its country of origin, and one that in China, whence Japan received this faith, has never played more than an episodic or secondary role. There is no contradiction here, in fact, but rather the expression of an inner polarity.

Only a man fettered, in the degree characteristic of the Japanese, to his society and to nature, living a cell-like life, chained to the wheel of birth and duty, family and state cult, worldly affairs and sentimental ties, can feel the full attraction of the Buddhist life of deliverance. "Bliss of all bliss, joy of all joy it is to leave behind the lie that says: 'I am'; no more henceforth do I cross the sea of life like some swimmer that wrestles with the waves in mortal agony; but, like the sea-gull in the huge swing of the law of cause and effect, without fear, unresisting, unafraid. This is the longed-for, supreme state of absolute equanimity, the elevation over all sorrow and joy, of earth and heaven; above youth and old age, health and sickness, life and death. This is the perfect vision of *Nibbhana* in this life. Such a one desires neither being nor non-being."[1]

It is not accidental that this nation of hero-worshippers has produced so few busts or statues of its great men, and that its best sculptors have devoted themselves to the profoundly antiplastic task of making images of saints who have withdrawn, or are in the act of withdrawing, from this world of form and name. Nor is it fortuitous that Japanese literature has produced many ballads and epic tales of chivalry (though no heroic epic) and many books of history, collections of acute observations and erudite notes, but nothing even vaguely resembling Herodotus' account of the ways and fates of neighbouring peoples, or Plutarch's comparative biographies of the great men of two countries. Japan abounds in men with strong personality, if by that much abused term nothing else is meant but the identity of a distinctive character. But Japanese life does not tolerate an individual deciding to determine his own life from his own centre, freely acknowledging responsibilities imposed by objective norms of goodness, beauty and truth, but moved most deeply by the Pindaric demand: "Become what you are."

Being, essence, creation, formation, configuration (*Gestaltung*) are not the guiding stars of these adventurers on the sea of Indian thought: "For one who had disappeared there is no measure . . . He has nothing by which one can describe him . . . As a flame blown out by the wind he disappears and cannot be defined . . . As flowing rivers disappear in the ocean, quitting name and form, so the sage throwing off his name and form goes into the highest heavenly person."[2] What is greatest in Japanese art and poetry partakes of this spirit, even if, and precisely when, it speaks of things and events in this fleeting world.

CEREMONY AND ETIQUETTE

Civilisation in the Far East centres round ceremony and etiquette conceived as a ritual ordering life both in the human and non-human sphere. The Japanese have received this ritualistic conception of life and many of its everyday and festive expressions from China. But they have sifted, assimilated and modified the details of ceremonial behaviour, retaining much that has been superseded in China by later customs, and they have added elements that seem to have never existed in China, and which often belong to a much older stock of humanity, recalling the shaman rather than the mandarin. Still more significant is the unconscious logic that has led the Japanese to give ritual a different meaning and a different relation to the rest of their world, even while they still believed in walking in the paths prescribed by the canonical books of the Confucian tradition.

Chinese rituals were sacramental representations, recreations of cosmic models. Their purpose may have been originally to vanquish the forces of chaos by establishing order and light, harmony and hierarchical power. Later thinkers saw them as methods of civilising man, of imposing measure and discipline. Writing in the third century B.C., Hsun Ch'ing, the philosopher *par excellence* of ritual, declared: "In meeting and parting with people, in one's style of walking, if these are in keeping with ritual, there is beauty and refinement about them; if they are not, then they show arrogance, surliness, vulgarity, and a barbarous spirit. Thus it is that without ritual man cannot live, nor his business in life succeed, nor his states and families abide."³

This Chinese ritual was powerfully laid out in space; it delighted in majestic orderliness and symmetry; an elaborate configuration of gestures and styles, hymns and sacrifices, was performed at altars and in temples that were spatial symbols of cosmic laws, of great tectonic beauty and well-articulated imperial force.

In Japan all these spatial elements are reduced to a bare minimum. The most elaborate of Japanese rituals are of rustic simplicity compared with their Chinese counterparts. The reading of a *norito* (Shinto invocation), the purifying waving of a wand, bowing and praying, the presentation of plain gifts of the sea and the fields, a chaste sacral dance, some archery or wrestling performed in the shrine precinct: these are the typical features of Japanese ritual. Some other ceremonies take place in the interior of shrines, rites of great simplicity in the half-darkness of the most austere of buildings. More often the gods are carried around in the streets, not by priests but by the young men and boys of the quarter. They shoulder the sacred palanquins in which the gods have taken abode. The gods drive their bearers wherever their incalculable and therefore divine wills direct them, often making the ark crash into the frames of wooden houses, bringing thereby good fortune to their owners.

In China the accent is on *conformity*, obedience to the laws of the universe, the performance of what is orderly and appropriate by imitating the orderly and appropriate ways of the macrocosm. In Japan emphasis is laid on *spontaneous* action availing itself of a minimum of external lay-out, defying symmetry and demanding the ever-renewed effort to open oneself to the inflow of a divine presence that springs from the very beginning of the world. Here, communing with the gods does not mean imitating a model, but going back to one's origins. The Chinese mind finds its natural home in Space, the Japanese in Time. The one rests in the contemplation of order, the other in the impulse and tension of movement.

It would be misleading to identify the meaning of Chinese ritual with mere formalism. This is a tendency inherent in every kind of ceremony; in China it appears to have overshadowed for centuries the true meaning of ritual. To counteract it had been a central motive of Confucius, one of those rare men who transcend the limits of their own race, by fulfilling on a higher plane of existence what is most noble in it. Even in later times philosophers of his school tried to keep awake the feeling that only the good can sacrifice without desacralising the rite. But it is a long way from this logic of ritual to the Japanese belief in the virtue of spontaneous action, springing up from the unconscious, regardless of minute orderliness and prefigured harmonies.

THE TEA CEREMONY

It is the spirit of such spontaneous feeling, a harmony that *happens* instead of being established by conscious endeavour, which characterises the tea ceremony (*Cha-no-yu*), from which a higher Japanese etiquette and style have been derived since the Ashikaga epoch. It would be unwise to speak of it without citing Okakura Kakuzo's *Book of Tea*, perhaps the most charming and

8

the most revealing book written by a modern Japanese on Things Japanese.

> "The ceremony was an improvised drama whose plot was woven about the tea, the flowers and the paintings. Not a colour to disturb the tone of the room, not a sound to mar the rhythm of things, not a gesture to obtrude on the harmony, not a word to break the unity of the surroundings, all movements to be performed simply and naturally—such were the aims of the tea ceremony."[4]

The greatest of tea-masters, Sen Rikyu, concludes his Hundred Rules for *Cha-no-yu* with the advice: "Though you may cleave to these rules and sometimes break them, and though you don't take them seriously, don't quite forget them."[*]

The difference between conformity to well-defined rules of conduct and the spontaneous realisation of their true meaning is well illustrated by the famous anecdote of Sen Rikyu teaching his son the meaning of the tea-master's demand for spotless cleanliness. Rikyu was watching his son Shoan as he swept and watered the garden path. "Not clean enough", said Rikyu, when Shoan had finished his task; and he told Shoan to try again. After a weary and further hour's work, the son turned to Rikyu: "Father, there is nothing to be done. The steps have been washed for the third time, the stone lanterns and trees are well sprinkled with water, moss and lichens are shining with a fresh verdure; not a twig, not a leaf, have I left on the ground." "Young fool," chided the tea-master, "that is not the way a garden path should be swept." Saying this, Rikyu stepped into the garden, shook a tree and scattered over the garden gold and crimson leaves, scraps of the brocade of autumn.[5]

A geometrical array of lines, ideas or virtues makes the

---

[*] Sen Rikyu (1522–1591), also known as Sen-no-Soeki, became a favourite of Hideyoshi's. The latter is said to have desired Rikyu's daughter; but her father resisted Hideyoshi's overtures. It may have been on these grounds—rather than for alleged arrogance—that Hideyoshi ordered Sen Rikyu to commit *seppuku* (hara-kiri). Rikyu's last request was to be allowed to prepare tea in the ceremonial manner before his suicide. The request was granted. [Ed.]

Japanese feel as if shut off from the springs of life. He delights in asymmetry, in what seems to be done in a haphazard way, in sounds coming through an impenetrable night from an unknown source, and, most of all, in everything that suggests the dew and coolness of a virginal morning.

GODS AND MYTHS

The Japanese seem to care little for the mythical tales of sacred books and local legends, with the exception of those serving to establish claims to political rule. Those handed down in the Imperial collections of the eighth century have been treated with reverence because of their great age and Imperial patronage; but for the same reason they have been regarded with some diffidence. The *Nihongi* (720 A.D.) includes additions, from various sources, of parallel versions that often widely disagree.

God-tales seem to have preserved a certain degree of plasticity up to the Ashikaga age when the texts of *No* plays were established; since then, fossilisation has set in; no Japanese Aeschylus or Wagner has moulded myths and sagas according to his own spirit. Among the students of higher schools and universities I found no trace of interest in native myths. Country people usually know no legend connected with a local shrine. Among the archaic god-tales only those betraying a foreign origin are attractive and suggestive. Where a myth has grown, or has been modified, in Yamato, political purposes can easily be detected. Few gods have definite physiognomies.

The very life of Shinto is to be found not in a set of beliefs but in a definite way of acting: bowing quietly, reverently calling the gods by clapping hands and silent prayer after having purified one's hands, one's mouth and one's thoughts. Theologians speak of an act of communion between the soul of the worshipper and the god. But do the gods exist in any form other than in such acts of reverence? The monk Saigyo professed not to know whether gods were or were not present behind the curtain of the Shrines of Ise. But he admitted that reverential awe made his tears well forth ("although I do not know at all whether anything honourably deigns to be there"[6]). This is Japanese piety, agnostic and reverential, full of awe and lucidity.

Yoshida Kenko, a writer of the fourteenth century, observed in his *Tsure-tsure-gusa* ("Harvest of Leisure") that if a man assumes the attitude of praying, even without pious thought, piety will come to him by virtue of this gesture. The detached psychology of this *apercu* sounds strangely modern and would not have surprised, perhaps, a monk of the Buddhist Shingon Sect, with its belief in the magical value of cultic gestures. Here, as elsewhere, the Japanese seem to have retained traits dating from an epoch when gods were born of, and were dominated by, rites, the gods themselves being the property of priests (*kan-nushi*, "god-possessors"). The brandishing of a sacral *nusa* (a stick bearing paper and hemp streamers) in the act of purification, the reading of the Imperial Rescript on Education in a school ceremony, the minutely prescribed attitudes of an archer, and the drawing of a hem by a Kano artist, belong to the same world and serve similar purposes.

To the Chinese "sincerity", one of the supreme values of Eastern ethics, means "not to deceive oneself", or others: establishing harmony between one's inner being and one's behaviour. To the Japanese it spells readiness to discard everything that might hinder a man from acting wholeheartedly on the pure and unpredictable impulses that spring from the secret centre of his being, ferociously if need be, and often without regard to the code of etiquette and ceremony which for the Chinese embodied law, truth and order, patterned upon the Will of Heaven.

Those impulses emerge suddenly, like a thunderstorm, a tidal wave, or a cloud of plum blossom carried by the wind; they do not follow the Chinese cosmic model of alternating opposites. To the Japanese, gods are "powerful and swift". This formula was perhaps originally applied to evil spirits that once swarmed on the "painfully uproarious" earth before the Heavenly Deities sent heroes to prepare the country for the coming of their emperor-descendants. Since the Middle Ages the words, "powerful and swift", have come to characterise Japanese gods in general, good

and evil alike. There is a poem, for example, by the Meiji
Emperor which reads:

> "The devotion that consumes
>   My people
> Will be pleasant
> To the heart of the gods
> The powerful-swift ones."[7]

The Japanese distinguish in their gods a Mild Spirit (*nigi
mitama*) and a Fierce Spirit (*ara mitama*), anticipating the distinction established by Western philosophers between the light and
the dark face of God, the *numen numinosum* and the *numen
tremendum*. The mirror seems to be the symbol (*shin-tai*, god-
body) of the first; the sword, of the second. Although the mirror
seems to take precedence over the sword, the symbol of the Fierce
(or Rough) Spirit continues to exercise his natural power of
fascination and prestige. Most men are apt to believe and trust in
what is like them, dark and chaotic, rather than in luminous
perfection. The Japanese hold decisive vehemence in a cultic
veneration that seems to gratify one of the deepest urges of the
race.

In no other religion, save perhaps that of the Scythians, has
the religious veneration of the sword and the spear—powerful,
swift, lightning-like weapons—played a similar role. The *gohei*,
zig-zag shaped strips of paper or cloth hanging from a pole in
Shinto shrines, may have originated in sacrificial offerings, or in
images of the gods themselves or in other divine symbols, such
as trees or pyramids. But all this has been long forgotten. To the
Japanese the *gohei* are conductors of god-power; the gods descend
through them, into them. And it is scarcely fortuitous that their
strange zig-zag form, whatever the origin of the *gohei*, resembles
nothing so much as lightning.

HEAVEN

To the Chinese, "Heaven" was an embodiment, semi-abstract,

semi-concrete, of the principle of authority, order, hierarchy, benevolence, goodness—equally at work in the king, the lord, the father, and the master of the house. Motoori Norinaga, the most characteristically Japanese of Japanese scholars and the spiritual father of modern Japanese nationalism, calls this conception ridiculous*; to a Japanese, "Heaven" cannot be anything but the place where the High Gods dwell, the highest of whom are the ancestors of the imperial dynasty and, owing to a strange emotional extension, of the whole Japanese nation. The *Kojiki* and *Nihongi* contain a number of cosmological myths, remnants of earlier civilisations or late borrowings by priestly theologians, in which nobody takes any interest. The way in which the official collections present the myths, attempting neither to conceal nor to reconcile contradictions, would suffice to show that already in the eighth century they were treated with the polite scepticism and formal reverence characteristic of an aristocratic society little disposed to pay much heed to scribes and theologians and their bookish worries. Metaphysics have never stirred the intellectual passion of the Japanese; who tend to take pragmatist attitudes and are always eager to shorten the circuit from one action to another. Speculation, which has been termed "suspended action", is not allowed to flower into conceptual edifices of ambitious sublimity, apt to acquire a spiritual life of their own, emancipated from the demands of action. Japanese thought is anxious never to cut its own umbilical cord.

DYNASTIC CONTINUITY

The only Japanese nature myth of importance—the Hiding of the Sun-Goddess—deals significantly with a disturbance of cosmic events, the eclipse of the sun caused by the violence of the storm-

---

* Motoori Norinaga (1730–1801) worked for thirty-five years on his annotated edition of the *Kojiki* (*Kojiki-Den*—"Commentary on the *Kojiki*"). A determined critic of both Buddhism and Confucianism, Motoori Norinaga was indeed "the spiritual father of modern Japanese nationalism." [Ed.]

god.* The Japanese is not overawed by the regularity of stellar motions and seasonal changes, but by the uni-dimensional lineage of Heavenly and Terrestial sovereigns supposed to stretch in unbroken continuity from the creation of the world to its end. There are no cyclic periodicities and no recurring events as in Chinese historiography. The sequence of generations represents a motion, flowing here with greater, and there with less, intensity, gathering momentum or slowing down, apt to lose itself and to recapture its vigour by renewing its life from the sacred source from which it has sprung. Revolution and regeneration (*isshin*) are here synonymous. In China a dynasty whose cosmic vitality had been exhausted was replaced by a new house deserving to become invested with the vacarious government of the Realm ("under heaven"—*t'ien-hsia*). In Japan, a crisis means the re-transfer of power from unworthy delegates of the Emperor to the original of authority.

We are not concerned here with the historiographical problem: whether the dynastic continuity claimed by Japanese patriots has been a fact of history. Nor are we concerned with the question of how there could exist a belief in the unimpaired transmission of the solar blood, since most mothers of sovereigns were not themselves of the imperial family but belonged to the Fujiwara and other clans. In our present study we are only concerned with the different roles played by the categories of space and time, by the phenomena of cyclic regularity and arrow-like linear motion, in the Chinese and Japanese ideals of rule and authority.

These mental differences seem to be closely interwoven with a

---

* The famous legend recounts the story of Amaterasu's alarm at her brother's behaviour and her subsequent hiding in a cave. (Amaterasu = The Sun-Goddess; her brother, Susanowo = The Storm God). After she shut herself up in the cave the world was plunged in darkness. Whereupon the deities of Heaven assembled outside the cave. They erected a sacred tree. In its upper branches they placed a jewel and in the middle branches a mirror. Then one of the goddesses performed a ribald and indecent dance, causing her audience to roar with laughter. This aroused Amaterasu's curiosity, and she peeped out of the cave. She saw her reflection in the mirror, and this enticed her further out. One of the gods drew her out completely and forbade her to return to the cave. Light once more filled the world. [Ed.]

polarity of conceptions for which there are suggestive parallels in the Near East. In Egypt, as in Japan, the king is the bodily descendant of the Sun-deity, himself divine, a life-giver and the sole source of authority. In Babylon, as in China, the king is only entrusted vicariously by the god with the task of terrestial governing, and thus he may suffer deposition if he proves no longer fit to act as a proxy of the god; he is not the incorporation of divine substance; he is measured according to a norm which he can obey in greater or lesser strictness. The Egyptian king, like the Japanese *tenno*, has no norm outside himself: he is the very substance of all that is good, by virtue of the historical fact of his descent. In China, as in Babylon, the ruler has above him a half-spiritual, half-spatial, Heaven which invests and judges and disinvests him. *Incorporation*, therefore, is connected, profoundly, with a temporal idea. *Vicarious government* is connected with a spatial idea. The first is based on a historical line of facts (real or imaginary), the second rests on the idea of a simultaneous correspondence (real or imaginary).

CHINESE ORIGINS

These dualisms dominate the canonical accounts the Chinese and Japanese have given of the origin and deeds of their first rulers. It does not matter very much whether these myths are as old as the traditions of the two nations assert. The place accorded to these stories in the *Chou-king* and the *Kojiki* is sufficient reason for regarding them as typical expressions of fundamental differences.

The *Chou-king*, or Book of Documents which may date from the Chou to the Han period, with possible remnants from Shang archives, begins with a chapter entitled: *The Norm of Yao* (a mythical emperor who is supposed to have lived in the third millennium B.C.).

"If we examine the life of the ancient Emperor Yao, we find that he bears justly the title 'Of Great Merit'. He was always intent upon fulfilling his duty, very perspicacious, of perfect virtue, rare prudence, and all that naturally and without effort.

Serious and respectful, he knew how to yield and how to condescend. His influence and his fame reached the utmost borders of the Empire, unto the very limits of Heaven and Earth."

Everything, here, is seen under the dual aspect of norm and fulfilment. There is no mythical guarantee of the ruler's virtue. His authority is not based on his divine origin but on his claim to virtue. The book tells us how he cultivated first his own virtue, thereby becoming able to lead his own family to a life of concord, then all the families in his territory, and finally the people of all other territories. His signal act of authority is the commission given to astronomers to ascertain the course of the stars and to determine the appropriate dates for every kind of performance, in harmony with the "laws of wide Heaven". He declines to choose his own son as his successor: "Ah, he is a liar and bent upon quarrelling: can he be fit?" Two more candidates are discarded. At last he elects Chouen, a man born of a malign father and a mendacious mother, but a man who had succeeded in making his parents and his haughty brother live a life of concord and in preventing them from "committing major misdeeds".

All historical rulers of China have been either descendants of earlier rulers or founders of new dynasties. The story of Yao's choice of Chouen (perhaps an ethical reinterpretation and rationalisation of archaic succession rites in which the future king had to prove his superior magical virtue in a number of tests), gains, accordingly, a significance that would not accrue to it in an age of elected kings. With the greatest emphasis the claims of blood, of inherited substance, are denied. Virtue consists in knowing and imitating the laws of the universe; the State is built upon individuals who have perfected their character and have become thereby able to mould the rest of mankind by their influence, moving in concentric rings into a state of cosmic orderliness. No specific description is given of the land Yao governs, nor are the dates of his life mentioned: his rule is defined in terms of spatial extension.

JAPANESE ORIGINS

Of the foundation of the Yamato empire by Jimmu Tenno, the *Nihongi,* compiled in the second decade of the eighth century A.D., gives the following account:

"When he reached the age of forty-five, he addressed his elder brothers and children, saying: 'Of old, our Heavenly Deities Taka-mi musubi no Mikoto and Oho-hiru-me no Mikoto (another name for Amaterasu Omikami—Ed.) pointing to this land of fair rice-ears of the fertile reed-plain, gave it to our Heavenly Ancestor Hiko-ho-no ninigi no Mikoto. Thereupon Hiko-ho-no ninigi no Mikoto, throwing open the barrier of Heaven and clearing a cloud-path, urged on his super-human course until he came to rest. At this time the world was given over to widespread desolation. It was an age of darkness and disorder. In this gloom, therefore, he fortified justice, and governed this Western border. Our Imperial Ancestors and Imperial parents like Gods, like sages, accumulated happiness and amassed glory. Many years elapsed. From the date when our Heavenly Ancestor descended until now it is over 1,792,470 years. But the remote regions do not yet enjoy the blessings of Imperial rule. . . . Now I have heard from the Ancient of the Sea that in the East there is a fair land encircled on all sides by blue mountains. Moreover, there is one who flew down riding in a heavenly rock boat. I think that their land will undoubtedly be suitable for the extension of the Heavenly task, so that its glory should fill the universe. It is doubtless the centre of the World. The person who flew down was, I believe, Nihi-haya-bi. Why should we not proceed thither and make it the capital?' All the Imperial Princes answered and said: 'The truth of this is manifest. This thought is constantly present to our minds also. Let us go there quickly.' This was the year Kinoye Tora (51st) of the Great Year."[8]

I have cited a version given by the *Nihongi,* the second of the classical books of Imperial traditions, because it is written under the influence of Chinese models. The *Kojiki* version seems to follow more closely the traditions of native clan-mythologists, and here Jimmu's eloquent address is reduced to a few bold words of virile decision and command. Yet in spite of a great number of obvious echoes from the Chinese in phraseology and detail, the *Nihongi* version is separated from the *Chou King* chapter by a world of mental difference. In the Japanese story the accent is all on Tradition, Generation, History, Mission; date and place, age and situation, are strictly defined. The whole account is rendered in terms of Here and There and Now and Once, of movements, acts, remembering, pointing, agreeing, resolving.

The tale begins at a point, as it were, away from the central spot; it is dominated by a direction towards the centre, not from it; and the direction is prefigured in a mythical and genealogical precedent, and is justified by the task of establishing an empire promised by ancestral gods to their descendants. The centre of the universe, in this tale, is a goal, not the starting point; and the character of this universe is not orderliness and regularity: it is a fabulous world inhabited by unpredictable powers. Some of these had to be eradicated or subdued before Jimmu Tenno's ancestors were permitted to tread the soil they were to rule; he himself is guided and assisted in his conquest by strange divine messengers which ride on tortoises and shake their wings; by golden birds resting on the point of a spear, by magical swords that have descended from heaven. It is a world still full of malign spirits, bears, spiders, vapours; to fight and overcome them quick sudden movements are needed, and every crafty device and cunning ruse is permitted; what matters is only the choice of the sharpest weapon—and unfailing alertness.

NOTES

1   Paul Dahlke, *Buddhist Essays*, London, 1908, p. 96.
2   Mundaka Upanishad 3, 2, 8; quoted by Sir Charles Eliot, *Japanese Buddhism*, London, 1935, p. 44.

3 E. R. Hughes, *Chinese Philosophy in Classical Times*, London, 1942, p. 250.

4 Okakura Kakuzo, *The Book of Tea*, Sydney, 1932, p. 21.

5 *Ibid.*, p. 44.

6 Arthur Waley, *Japanese Poetry, the Uta*, London, 1919, p. 102.

7 Kurt Singer, "Ueber das japanische Gedicht", *Die Neue Rundschau*, Amsterdam, 1949, no. 16, p. 556 *et seq.*

8 W. G. Aston, *Nihongi*, London, 1896, pp. 110–111.

8

Calligraphy, Poetry and Zen

CALLIGRAPHY

Japan's indebtedness to China is most patent in her use of the Chinese script, those strangely attractive ideograms, partly pictorial and partly phonetically used, which have added so much to the aesthetic charm of Far Eastern civilisation, while acting as a powerful brake on its intellectual development. When the Japanese became acquainted with the *kanji* (Chinese script) at the latest in the fifth century A.D., they had no script of their own invention, except, perhaps, rune-like marks of doubtful origin and age. They have treasured the precious and Pandorean gift with the fervour of an acolyte; considering it inappropriate to destroy a single sheet of paper on which ideograms have been drawn. To this day an inordinate amount of time is devoted to the learning of several thousands of these characters, thus preventing the child from applying its mind to less mechanical tasks and furthering a certain tendency to care for accuracy of detail, meticulously copied, and for seductive elegance in overcoming the hardness of rigid lines by swift and wilful strokes of the brush, which leave the reader something to admire and, still more, to puzzle over.

Many modern Japanese have deplored the burden thrown upon their minds by their fidelity to the Chinese script. It may be asked, however, whether it was solely the deadweight of tradition which made them cling to a way of writing that had fewer advantages for the small insular kingdom than for the immense agglomeration of the parts of the Chinese Empire, with their populations so vastly differing in pronunciation that an alphabetic or syllabic script would have made literary intercourse in the native tongue between the various provinces an impossibility.

In Japan the *kanji*, in addition to their unquestionable aesthetic interest, must have answered to other tastes and purposes—to the Japanese preference for what is hazy, well-shrouded, capable of more than one meaning; and to the technique of a patriarchal government which would feel much embarrassed if everybody could read everything with as much ease as the Western alphabet allows. The argument, which is often heard, that the Japanese language, with its wealth of homonyms, would become incomprehensible, if phonetic writing should be allowed to prevail, seems to carry less weight: by the introduction of new diacritical signs and suitable composite words these difficulties could be overcome without causing too much lack of elegance; nor would the charm of Japanese life be seriously disturbed if Japanese talking to one another were no longer under the necessity of clarifying the meaning of their oral communications by sketches of ideograms drawn with the finger of one hand on the palm of the other.

In fact the Japanese a thousand years ago had already introduced into their writing system an important element not of Chinese origin, and well adapted to the peculiar character of the Japanese language: the two syllabaries of *kata-gana* and *hira-gana*. The supporters of the theory of a Chinese hegemony over Japanese culture appear to overlook the fact that the creation of these well-constructed and handy signs (attributed to the great Buddhist teacher Kobo Daishi, who may have utilised Sanscrit script*) and their welding together with the Chinese ideograms was no mean achievement; it permitted unambiguous writing for words without a Chinese equivalent, and it gave scope for the free development of Japanese syntax and

---

* Kobo Daishi is the posthumous, sacred, name of the Abbot Kukai (774–835), famous as a saint, artist, and calligrapher; the founder of the Shingon sect of Buddhism. [Ed.]

accidence, which follow laws very different from those governing the Chinese language. Chinese is marked by a general lack of inflexional affixes and by a very limited use of auxiliaries. Japanese, an agglutinative language, delights in auxiliaries, amplifies determinators, and has a much ampler store of prepositions and conjunctions. These characteristic elements are written, for the most part, in *kana*; they gave to Japanese a plasticity denied to Chinese, which demands a rigid order of words. There is no more significant index of the creative force of a nation than its language. Japanese, with all its merits and limitations and in spite of some affinities with Ugro-Finnish and other tongues, is not modelled upon any foreign pattern.

Even in the delineation of Chinese characters the Japanese have developed a style of their own which Chinese critics are accustomed to distinguish and willing to appreciate; they do not set much value on Japanese scrolls written in the typically Chinese manner, but find a beauty all their own in *kakemono* scrolls written in the heterodox Japanese style.

Calligraphy, the art of drawing characters in writing a book, a poem, a letter, a script—not only obeying the laws of felicitous communication of facts and purposes, but also expressing the mind and soul and spirit of the writer—may be said to embody the quintessence of Far Eastern art, Chinese as well as Japanese. Perhaps the decorative use to which calligraphic scrolls are put originated in a reflex from Islamic culture, which reached China during the T'ang period, the Moslems being forbidden by their religion to make images of living beings, and thus induced to find a congenial expression of their motor-minded souls in the medium of abstract forms animated by mental associations. In China this art may have come as a resurrection of those archaic moods which have bred the a-plastic, non-realistic patterns of the earliest bronzes, expressions of primeval attitudes of the Chinese soul.

The Japanese introduced not only the forms of Chinese ideograms but also the aesthetic code of the Chinese art of writing. They copied the script of the famous masters, as only Japanese are able to copy—observing minutely the smallest details and following these models for centuries with the zeal of a penitent monk or an athlete in training. Yet anyone gifted with an aesthetic sense of abstract forms and rhythms, who has an opportunity of seeing good specimens of Chinese and Japanese calligraphy exhibited on the walls of the same room, will feel a difference great enough to make him wonder whether the Chinese and Japanese exhibits belong to the same world. They are almost as incommensurable as a sonnet of Petrarca and a bar of Debussy's music. They resemble each other only in the common quality of being alien to Western aesthetics of writing, with its demand for plastic definiteness and lucid articulation. The Chinese and Japanese aim is not to reproduce in a more graceful or more majestic manner standardised forms of letters which remain unchanged by their context, but to melt down these self-contained units into a spontaneous flow of motion. Motion, however, in Chinese art and motion in Japanese art would seem not to have the same meaning.

CHINESE CALLIGRAPHY

A piece of Chinese writing, however strictly it may avoid geometrical symmetry, conveys to the eye (and through the eye to the whole body) the sense of perfect equipoise. The single characters may be shaped in bold asymmetry, but they do balance. They speak of a world in which no preference is given to day or night, acting or suffering, great or little, male or female, heaven or earth, not because of a placid indifference (which seems to characterise the Chinese only in their periodically recurring states of confusion and lassitude) but by reason of a belief in a cosmic law which unites opposites in a rhythmical sequence of alternating states, aspects, patterns of universal life. That cosmic law is not a matter of mere rational speculation or mystic introversion: it expresses itself in bodily movements, postures, gestures; and nowhere is to be felt more irresistibly than in a perfect Chinese song or dance—forms which were, in their beginning, inseparable. Lin Yutang was right in calling the "grass script" style of

Chinese calligraphy not a "running" but a "dancing" script.[1] The brush moves according to its own laws, free from any meretricious intention to imitate external models, but it leaves an impression of dancers; balancing, swinging, parting, calling each other, opposing each other, and reuniting in a finale that resolves antagonism in unison and preserves tension in harmony.

The Chinese insist, and insist aptly, upon the axiom that motion, flow, rhythm are the very life of calligraphy. But in their art this self-generating rhythm ends by representing a universe. The images and memories of things living in the mind of the artist may be transformed, transfigured, enchanted; they may be submerged by cascades and whirlpools: but they persist in sending the niceties of their forms and colours to the surface of the waters, like pebbles, fishes, or weeds shining with unearthly lustre from the bottom of a clear, deep stream.

An author of the T'ang Dynasty has noted such impressions in a passage of singular precision and grace:

"Here a drop of crystal dew hangs its ear on the top of a needle. There, the rumble of thunder hails down a shower of stones. I have seen flocks of queen swans floating on their stately wings. Or a frantic stampede rushing off at a terrific speed. Sometimes, in the lines a flaming Phoenix dances a lordly dance, or a sinuous serpent wriggles with speckled fright. And I have seen sunken peaks plunging headlong down the precipices, or a person clinging on a dry vine while the whole silent valley yawns below. Some strokes seem as heavy as the falling banks of clouds, others as light as the wings of a cicada. A little conducting and a fountain bubbles forth, a little halting and a mountain settles down in peace. Tenderly a new moon beams on the horizon; or, as the style becomes solemn a river of stars, luminous and large, descends down the solitary expanse of the night."[2]

The Chinese draw not only their imagery from the world of objects, but also their technical terms. They speak of the "muscles", "bones", "sinews" of the stroke. Other terms are

9

taken from the sphere of statics: the characters are called "structures", some "toppling", some "counter-balancing", some with
"lower support", some "facing inwards", or "facing outwards".
If, in this art, objects and beings are reduced to motion, it is a
motion in which their structural law, the pattern of their spatial
existence, is transparent.

JAPANESE WRITING

The writing art of Japan, after the task of acquiring the foreign
technique has been mastered and the writer feels free to follow
his own nature, does not reveal the laws of objects; it represents
what must be called, for want of a better term, absolute motion—
the movements of a soul possessed by a magic power which makes
it advance and hesitate, rush and slacken, lose and find itself again,
gather momentum and softly fade away; it reminds us of the dances
of North-east Siberian shamans which seem to survive exquisitely
sublimated in the *Nō*-play dances of Japan. If Japanese calligraphy
seems to suggest any features of the external world, it is the image
of lightning, of a cyclone, or the dripping of autumn rain. Chinese
writing can often be interpreted as a drama of conflicting forces.
It should not be impossible to find Chinese characters written in
such a way that their dramatic rhythms and tensions evoke the
rhythmical pattern of *King Lear, Coriolanus, Measure for Measure*.
Japanese characters are not dramatic but monodic, and their
beauty is linear rather than two- or three-dimensional.

Where these patterns of abstract motion seem to convey a
human message, it is the determination and the despondency,
the flight and the resignation of the solitary soul of which they
speak; or it is the bare flux of life which makes exaltation glide
into despair, joy rise imperiously out of sullen numbness, and
fits of melancholy mingle with a cry of triumph. The Japanese
style is essentially an art of transitions, glidings, subtle joinings,
and bewildering starts. I do not know whether a book on the
aesthetics of calligraphy has ever been written by a Japanese in
which these distinctive traits are stressed. Perhaps in this, as in

so many other fields, the Japanese have kept on repeating foreign formulas, with unfeigned reverence, in the belief that they act upon them, unconscious of the fact that long ago they had begun to move in another direction.

The difference between the two styles of writing seems to assert itself even in the elementary details of technique. The Chinese calligrapher generally guides the brush in a plane perpendicular to the writing material. The Japanese apparently apply it much more frequently at an oblique angle.[3] What else could have led these zealous pupils to deviate from models held in quasi-religious veneration but the instinctive knowledge that only by departing from the vertical plane can the impulse of movement be given its maximum of freedom from the rigid pattern of symmetry and balance?

SONGS AND DANCES

The essence of motion, as conceived by the Japanese, will be understood best if an attempt is made to sing an ancient Japanese tune and to perform the measures of a characteristic traditional dance. Neither follows a metrical scheme. They do not know that tension between the free flow of rhythm and the arithmetics of a metre from which song and dance in Europe draw vitality and charm, and they are never carried away by the autonomous power of a metrically rhythmic pattern. In Japan, song and dance seem to require at every moment new impulses, stimulations, "*Innervationen*", and a constant readiness to obey a sudden change of direction and tempo. The impulses governing movement seem to take little account of the body's natural inclinations and aversions, characteristics of a physical structure which is, after all, not perfectly fitted for response to the *élan vital* in its primordial purity.

A Japanese dance or song seldom allows one to surrender to that rhythmic balancing prefigured in the design of the human body. There are no repetitions, no returns to the beginning, no variations of a basic pattern. At any moment the most unexpected, the most difficult, the most anti-organic movement is likely to be made, but always, if the thing is well done, with apparent ease and the charm peculiar to things of great difficulty performed as if they were the effortless improvisations of a felicitous, happy, nature—the gift of a choice hour in which the improbable is allowed to happen.

This miracle is achieved by strictly resisting any temptation to relax, allowing the body to fall back into those rocking, bending, balancing movements which seem prefigured in the happy configuration of our anatomy and physiology, the laws of gravitation, and the framework of three-dimensional space. These songs and dances may be called essentially "magical" if we define magic, with a late classical writer (was it Macrobius?), as "the art which goes contrariwise to Nature". Most of the archaic songs and dances of Japan arose from spells, incantations, exorcisms, and oracles: they served to call gods, to expel demons, to save and to heal. Were not the Japanese mystics and poets of later ages merely transferring to another sphere the forces that gave life to these magic formulas? Nichiren, the most Japanese among the great Buddhist teachers of the Kamakura period, imperiously demanding to see the whole of Buddhism in the *Lotus Scripture* and this whole scripture contained, moreover, in its title alone, five magic syllables embodying for him the entire saving power of the Enlightened One; or that painter of the Tokugawa age who knew how to put all the strength of his soul into one long-drawn perpendicular stroke in painting a bamboo stalk; or the haiku poet Basho divining in a single movement or sound the meaning of life ("an old temple pond; a frog jumping; noise of the water"*); or the Zen monk attesting to the attainment of truth in the mere act of striking, jumping, shouting—all these are definite expressions of the same magic-minded and acosmic attitude.

---

* Matsuo Basho (1644–1694) is generally regarded as the greatest of haiku poets; and the haiku quoted by Singer is probably the best known of all haiku poems in Japan. [Ed.]

MYTH AND MAGIC

Chinese art and thought, too, emerge from a magical matrix full of perilous forces, fraught with terror and destruction, challenging the mind of man to subdue the uncontrollable by means of formulas, rites, and dances: some of these, long extinct in their country of origin, are still performed at the Imperial Court of Japan side by side with rites of indigenous origin. But there has never been an attempt made to revive in Japan those most peculiar forms of archaic Chinese religion and art of which the *T'ao t'ieh* is the supreme instance: an image of the image-less Power which is in the heart of this magic world, a system of pre-human, pre-cosmic "force lines", the diffused mystery of the cruel truth behind all cosmic order and beauty. The Japanese do not realise the evil forces of this world as a spatial pattern, to be visualised in a tangle of lines out of which a terrifying mask is going to emerge. They are satisfied that by virtue of the divine qualities of their ancestors these forces have been vanquished; the dreadful era in which the "rocks and tree stumps were talking" has been closed; the heart of man is pure; it does not know of those terrible propensities which the Chinese recognised in the *T'ao T'ieh* mask. Incantations and rites serve to banish the polluting influences which may linger on here and there, washing them down into the bottom of the sea; or they may serve to invite the gods to take their abode with men, share their pleasure and renew their own pristine vigour and purity.

CHINESE POEMS

The classical Chinese poem is built up in perfect symmetry. No symmetry could be more charming than that of the couplets and quatrains of the T'ang poems which recall the dual image of a scene and its mirrored counterpart on the surface of a lake—causing you to wonder which of the two images is the real one, the upper with its more definite outlines, or the lower with its refreshed colours. More than one millennium ago stern laws of cosmic equilibrium had been enunciated in the sacred books of China, represented in the ceremonial of state cult, and cast into the imperative shape of bronze vessels used in religious ritual. The essence of those laws seems to have been distilled by the T'ang poets; in their works the archaic pattern has acquired an airy lightness, unworldly subtlety, a dreamy fugitiveness alien to classical Chinese culture. Yet the newly acquired Buddhist sense of the impermanence of things has not quite annihilated the indigenous belief in the massive rights of the here and now, in the beauty of matter, in a sensual spell.

In the spirit of the T'ang poems both worlds hold each other in a subtle balance, and the technique of these stanzas of two quatrains mirrors this balance in the laws governing their sequences of "soft" and "hard" monosyllables. A system of permutation leads an initial pattern finally back to its beginning. No poem of eight lines could hope to achieve more beauty and finality.

JAPANESE POETRY

The Japanese have at an early date learnt to write such Chinese poems, much as European writers have for centuries sought pleasure and distinction in writing Latin and Greek verses in the classical languages, or applied to their mother-tongue the metres and forms of antiquity. In doing so the Japanese, to this day, have followed a curious self-imposed law. They not only obey strictly the severe Chinese rules of rhymes and word-sequences but also they treat as rhymes only those words which actually rhymed in China many centuries ago. In the meantime the written characters have acquired quite different sound values both in China and Japan. Rhyming words—that is to say, words which rhymed in Chinese when the rules of poetry were laid down—do not rhyme when the characters are read by Japanese: the observance of such rules is therefore devoid of aesthetic significance. Already in the T'ang era, when the Japanese learned these poems, many of these words rhymed no longer, even for Chinese ears. For a Japanese the contrast between the difficulties created by strict adherence to the canon and the aesthetic effects realised must have been incomparably greater, but they continued to remain loyal to that code. The phenomenon may remind us of the reluctance of early man to change the least detail of a ceremony, from fear that any such change might impair its magical efficacy. The actual motive, however, seems to have been the Japanese dread of incurring the slightest reproach of not strictly obeying the rules of the game; and there was the dread of being ridiculed for being second-rate, unskilled, or badly informed.

On the whole, the practice of writing Chinese verses over a dozen centuries seems to have produced in Japan as little poetry of the first order as the writing of Latin verses did in Western Europe. The main stream of Japanese poetry springs from another source and follows autochthonous laws. The Japanese have submitted most of their archaic poetry to the discipline of alternating lines of five syllables and seven syllables, a pattern borrowed from certain Chinese verses. But at an early date they added another seven-syllable line, making for asymmetry. A poem of this pattern is not intended to be danced, nor can it be visualised as a symmetrical image: it has a one-dimensional movement animated by a growing tension which is released in the last line, like an arrow leaving the sinew of a bow.

Indeed, the five lines of such a poem may be compared with the five motions of Japanese ceremonial archery: the calm setting up of the bow; its solemn raising; the slow drawing of the bow-string at the eye level; and the release of the shaft. This is more than a metaphor. The Japanese hold the arrow in cultic veneration, a heritage from very early stages of mankind. An arrow is enshrined as god-body (*shintai*) at some of the most powerful sanctuaries; ceremonial archery is practised in the shrine precincts at many festivals; and generation by an arrow is the sure mark of divine origin in more than one Japanese genealogy of rulers.

VISION AND MOVEMENT

We have dwelt at some length on differences of rhythm, which is the soul of poetry. To show the same contrasts in the matter of content, in the material substrata of ideas and images entering the texture of a poem, is an easy task. There can be no doubt that the most significant of Chinese poems evoke a visual impression, or a sequence of such images. They are pictures in words. The Japanese poem does not so much evoke a world of form and colour as embody movement. It recalls the swinging of a bough that a bird has just left, or the flight of wild geese about to disappear in the clouds, or the inexorable thrust of a blade towards the body. The Chinese poet allows himself to dwell on an enchanting scene until, like the magic mountain in a well-known Chinese fairy tale, it opens and draws him into it so that he is seen no more. To the Japanese every sight is but a springboard. Where the Chinese may find repose it is not given to the Japanese to pause; where the Chinese poet achieves self-realisation, the Japanese awaits the signal that bids him start on his journey.

FINE ARTS

The products of fine arts, more closely tied to the realm of matter than poetry by the laws of their technique and by the choice of their subjects, bear also more openly the marks of foreign models and borrowings. The sculpture of Greece, the architecture of Rome, the paintings of Italy and France, have left more obvious traces of influence on contemporary and later followers abroad than their poetry and music; yet those marks are far from telling the whole tale. If Japan had lacked creative genius, as a widespread opinion would have it, we should see her painters and sculptors not only following Chinese models and tendencies, but also proving unable to impress these forms with a spirit of their own. This has not been so.

Of pupilage on a grand scale there can be no doubt. It was China who taught Japan her first steps in painting and sculpture. China transmitted wave after wave of continental influences throughout the history of Japanese fine arts and was regarded by Japanese artists as the half-mythical country of beauty and wisdom "across the seas". Sung pictures were the most coveted treasures of the Ashikaga rulers and their circle (in which the aesthetic standards of Japanese culture crystallised). A Japanese "Chinese School" of painting (*Kanga*) furnished the official art of the Tokugawa Shogunate; not only was the technique of Chinese painting adopted, but also Chinese subjects and motives were given precedence and Chinese scenes were thought more worthy of being portrayed than those of the Japanese islands with all their subtle charm. There is a striking parallel here with the veneration in which Greece and Italy and their arts were held by later generations in Western and Central Europe. In Japan, however, the phenomenon is intensified by an Oriental inclination to extol one's masters and all that is ancient, hiding one's own pride behind a ceremonial veil of respect and self-denigration.

This peculiar trait has often misled unwary foreign observers; for there is often a failure to distinguish in a work of art between its material aspects (technique and subject matter), which are accessible even to persons of slight aesthetic sensibility, and those qualities that require an artist's insight. Shakespeare took the plots of many plays from Italian writers or from Plutarch; many of Beethoven's melodic themes were not his own invention; German Gothic architecture largely depended on French precedents. In the sphere of art and poetry perfection ranks higher than inventiveness, and to infuse a mass of tradition hallowed by age, and bearing the mark of strong predecessors, with a spirit of one's own is no mean achievement. In point of fact, the common fallacy of denying strength and originality to Japanese artists is not shared by any competent historian of Oriental art.

LANDSCAPE-PAINTING AND ZEN

Landscapes in black and white, dreamy lakes with returning or resting fishing boats, lofty mountains disappearing in veils of clouds, romantic gorges animated by rushing torrents or waterfalls, the dwellings of meditative hermits and roving poets, hamlets perched in the snow; all this painted in a visionary style, in bold and delicate strokes of a brush unwilling to follow palpable contours in a realistic manner—what kind of meaning do these pictures convey? What motives have determined the choice of these landscapes and of this ink-wash technique? An answer is ready at hand. The greatest works of this school, dating from the Ashikaga period in Japan and the Sung era in China, are dominated by the Buddhism of the Zen sect, with its cult of boldness and simplicity, its doctrine of the irrelevance of dualistic concepts, including good and evil, self and the external world, life and death; its resolute will to disregard traditions and authorities, cult and dogma; its fervent and reckless determination to reach the unknowable, call it Nought or Absolute.

There can be no doubt that Chinese landscape painting of this *suiboku* type was brought from China to Japan by Zen monks. Some of the greatest Japanese masters of this school, Shubun and Sesshu above all, were adepts of this sect.* It is less certain that the most famous among the Chinese *suiboku* masters were inspired by this mysticism, which bears more resemblance to the teaching of the Vedanta than to Buddhism proper. There have been Zen masters in the T'ang and later Sung period, like Mu Ch'i and Liang K'ai, and these have found many followers in Japan: not less strong, however, has been the influence of Ma Yuan and Hsia Kuei, who cannot be cited as torch-bearers of Zen mysticism. Still less can the most representative Chinese landscape painter of the Sung period, Kuo Hsi, and his school be regarded as Zen artists.

If an artist is a man for whom, in the words of Théophile Gautier, "the phenomenal world (*le monde sensible*) exists", Kuo Hsi and most of the great painters of the Northern Sung period have been artists indeed. Landscape, for them, was not a mere symbol hinting at the Absolute which is beyond form and colour and being, an invitation to withdraw conveyed by mountains

---

* *suiboku-ga* are monochrome paintings in tonalities of black India-ink. The fifteenth-century Buddhist priest and painter, Shubun (dates of birth and death uncertain), Abbot of Shokokuji Temple, was the teacher of Sesshu (1420-1506), commonly regarded as the greatest master of Japanese *suiboku* painting. [Ed.]

that have lost their substance, by birds flying and boats gliding into a void. "Among landscapes," writes Kuo Hsi in his great treatise in which the convictions of classic Chinese landscape painting have been codified, "there are those fit to walk through, those fit to contemplate, those fit to live in." Nature is not to be annihilated but must be shown in her moods and motions.

"Mountains are big things; their shape may be high and lofty, proud and arrogant, dignified and genuine; they may be as if seated with laps spread out or with legs crossed. . . . They may be massive and thick, bold and brave; they may reveal a living spirit, and be majestic and strong. They may be as if looking around or bowing in salutation. They may have a crown on the top and a seat below, a support in front and something to lean on at the back. They may be looking down as if observing something, or strolling about waving like banners. . . . The mountains have the water-course as their arteries, grass and trees as their hair; mists and clouds are their complexion. Therefore mountains must have water to be alive, grass and trees to be beautiful, mist and clouds to be fine and alluring."[4]

For this art, Nature is a living macro-organism composed of micro-organisms, each sharing the same immense powerful life. Mountains move like snakes, trees stretch out hands, waves are dancing, for "water is a living thing". This is, if any philosophic formula can be applied, pantheism inspired by anthropomorphic "empathy", not the spirit of the nought boldly denying the relevance of anything capable of being perceived by the senses and formulated in concepts. Professor Grousset, in his interpretation of early Sung art, was wise in citing not the famous Zen sutras but the poems of the T'ang era. "When things do not go in harmony with his desire in this life, man can but cast himself into a boat and drift with blown hair at the caprice of the waves", sings Li T'ai-po. "To build a terrace in deserted land and enjoy from it the purity of the evenings; to watch the rain veiling the heavy foot of the clouds, while the light bodies of the swallows are borne away on the wind", is the ideal of Sung Po-jin. "I am like a frail barque," confesses To-fu, "bound to the shore by a chain": he longs to see the desolate face of autumn and "to feel oneself a stranger wherever one may go".[5] This is exquisite, but it is not Zen.

The Zen monk does not feel a stranger; he has come home. He does not soar towards a world of clouds, for the Absolute is in him; he does not leave his hut, nor is he tempted to float adrift: in conquering the realm of being and non-being, virtue and vice, law and lawlessness, he has found a new determination, rock-like, unshakeable. It is this interior source of firmness and fearlessness which is the soul of the paintings of Shubun and Sesshu. It is not enough to point to the stronger character, individuality, and definiteness of form of the Japanese landscapes: their spirit differs from that of their Chinese models and masters by the intensity of just that feeling that may be expected to spring from genuine Zen training. These Japanese pictures are not quietist and contemplative; they do not invite to withdraw; they only show nature and man gliding back into the Realm of the Nought, in order to sally forward with a new power of decision and intransigence. Mountains and waters, trees and houses are not on the point of vanishing but are, as it were, *in statu nascendi*. Nature, here, is an almost unspatial, or pre-spatial, field of forces breaking into being, in violent tension and pregnant with indomitable energies.

Even in the work of Mu Ch'i and Liang K'ai, certainly great members of the Chinese Zen school of painting, the ancient legacy of Chinese thought and art is never lost—its sense of equipoise, its all-pervading sense of space, its vision of a whole conceived as a receptacle of balancing, half-material, half-spiritual, forces. Any image, however cloud-like, dissolving, ethereal, however close it comes to an intimation of mysterious realms and beings, yet remains an element in a spatial universe. Forms are caressing each other, consoling each other, holding each other by the hands in fraternal tenderness. In some of the most significant works of the Japanese *suiboku* school the world seems to be just emerging from a pre-cosmic state, in which there are neither things nor dimensions nor tangible masses, but only fields of magnetic currents generating a sequence of unpredictable motions, tensions, outbreaks of light and form.

It is not an accident that China has repudiated her best Zen artists; their works were brought to Japan at an early date and must be studied in the monasteries of Kyoto and in other Japanese collections. Mu Ch'i, Professor Siren notes, is almost forgotten in his own country. Chinese critics observe that "he painted in a coarse and repellent fashion not in accordance with the ancient rules and really not for refined enjoyment". Similar judgments have been passed on Liang K'ai.[6]

Zen Buddhism flourished in China, in a period of defeat and retirement during the Southern Sung era, in a few monasteries in the Lake region of South Central China. It may have contributed towards making a number of individuals serene and aloof in the midst of troubles and destruction and poverty; on the fate of the Chinese Empire it appears to have had no lasting effect. After fleeing to Japan, the same monks, by their teaching and their attitude, became the spiritual guides of the later Kamakura Shogunate (more precisely the Hojo Regency). To the moral strength imparted by the new discipline Japanese historians attribute the calm determination with which the Hojo faced and averted the Mongol danger. In the mental history of man there are few things more worth pondering than the fact that a meditative school coming from India, and leaving only episodic traces on Chinese civilisation, should have become, once it was transferred from China to Japan, the source of a moral and aesthetic culture expressing the most Japanese among Japanese qualities.

It is in Sesshu, the leading artist of the Ashikaga period and one of those few men of genius in whom a nation finds supreme expression by transcending its own limitations, that the true spirit of the Zen school has achieved its highest artistic aspirations, combining boldness and simplicity, free both from the slavish imitation of external objects and from the escapist content of vague suggestions, impressionist intimations and soothing unrealities. He combines, in the manner of earlier Japanese masters of the Yamato-e school, "soft" and crisp elements within one picture in order to produce a maximum of tension, life and stirring energy.

These landscapes have nothing romantic about them. The scenes portrayed are ordinary and familiar; even the menacing grandeur of Shubun's perpendicular rocks, living symbols of transcendent sublimity, is absent, or remains gently veiled in the background. The pictures possess in the highest degree the quality termed in Japanese *meikai* (openness, directness). Their mystery is the secret not of the rare and hidden things but of what is ordinary and contained in the *haecceitas* ("such-ness") of things (as scholastic philosophers called in barbaric Latin the quality by virtue of which a thing is just what it is).

Chinese landscapes have an aspect of universality not bound to a specific time and place; the same is true of their portraits of saints and monks. As soon as this kind of painting becomes acclimatised in Japan it changes its character: localities and personalities become sharply individualised. There are no more mountains and rivers "in general": the demands of the Here and Now are strictly fulfilled. Action—the soul of this most detached of styles—calls for concrete determination of space and time.

If one compares Chinese and Japanese pictures seeming to treat the same "subjects", or even when they appear to stand in the relation of model and variation, it is surprising how static, quiet, soothing, Chinese versions seem beside their Japanese counterparts. Chinese birds seem to hover in the air, flowers expand into a geometric pattern, space is a homogeneous volume filled with substance. In Japanese landscapes and in their bird and flower paintings, trees and branches tend to take the configuration of forked lightning, and orchids break a hard stone with the élan of a sword thrust. There are few Chinese landscape scenes which do not invite the spectator to dwell there, rain or no rain, storm or no storm. Very few Japanese landscape paintings convey this desire; but they force and hold the eye with the magic of leaping flames and furrowed seas and unruly hair, of swift processes in the retorts of a chemical laboratory, and of the stir and movement of soldiers breaking up a camp, bound to march on, to a destination unknown.

DESCENT

It is not given to men to endure the power of mystery and ecstasy for more than brief spaces of time. The terrifying aloofness of Shubun, the volcanic energy of Sesshu binding itself to what is ordinary, are softened by followers and friends and gradually adapted to the moods of lesser men; the elements of firmness and dream, tension and self-abandonment, dissociate themselves; revelation becomes subjective expression, symbols degenerate into genres; the wine of intuition is filled in to the vessels of tradition, ready to be used by lesser hands and coarser minds, but flaring up again in purer souls that break flame-like the darkness of life on its decline. It was a high achievement of the painting of the Tokugawa period to keep so much of the Ashikaga legacy alive, in forms more or less standardised and accessible to artists of lesser power.

The memorable fact that during the Tokugawa period Japanese art, unlike poetry and literature, did not congeal into formalism and lose itself in non-artistic pursuits, was largely due to the infusion into the official schools of a native tradition of painting, *Yamato-e,* which since its origin, not later than the Fujiwara period, had remained singularly free from continental impulses and models. Combining an exquisite sense of bold decorative design and colour with an intense grasp of rapid motion and individual expression, the *Yamato-e* has produced an uninterrupted stream of original works; and these, like the best *tanka* and *haiku* poems, and in a spirit akin to the works of Murasaki Shikibu and Sei Shonagon, reveal the innermost gifts and stirrings of the Japanese race. The *Yamato-e* moves with equal lightness of touch, natural elegance and child-like enjoyment, in the realms of legend and of everyday life; it is equally true to itself in scrolls depicting the life of saints and the routine of court ladies. It was the colour-prints of the later Tokugawa age—the last flash of the *Yamato-e*—which first made Western eyes acquainted with Japanese art. The classic works of the *Yamato-e,* which date from the twelfth and thirteenth centuries, are still known to only few Western students. With their audacious slanting lines, with their freedom from convention and realism alike, and their vivifying candour and power, they reveal much of what the Japanese understand life to be at the best moments granted by this "fleeting world".

HOUSES

The Japanese preference for the asymmetrical is related to their love of the Not Quite Finished, the Not Altogether Perfect—a tendency sometimes carried to bizarre and artificially primitive extremes. But it is more than a matter of taste, and even more than a conventionalised application of Taoist wisdom: it seems to spring from the primary instincts of life conceived as pure motion and thus hostile to a perfection that leaves no room for desire. Faust dies when he is urged to ask the instant to stay: "*Verweile doch, du bist so schön!*"

Nothing speaks more distinctly and unerringly of the soul of a nation than the style of its houses. However much be due to the differences of climatic conditions in China and Japan, resulting in the one country in solid structures made of stone, tile and mud, and in the other in the lightest kind of wood construction (which seems to perpetuate the principles of Stone Age pile-work), the demand for perfect symmetry in China, for strict asymmetry in Japan, cannot be fully explained by external factors. The Japanese copied Chinese architecture at an early date. But already in the seventh century, a period governed by strong Chinese influences, the Horiuji Temple, near Nara, broke deliberately with the law of symmetry in the arrangement of its two main buildings. The great shrine of Izumo, although showing distinct traces of Sino-Buddhist models in some details, has yet the bold asymmetrical ground-plan of the Japanese peasant house. Aristocratic mansions, which during the "middle ages" followed Chinese designs, have since the Ashikaga period avoided bilateral balance and, with equal strictness, every curved line—with the exception of one circular window, placed asymmetrically, near the corner of a guest room or by a staircase. Only the four-and-a-half-mat tearoom, as designed by Rikyu, is arranged almost symmetrically, the mats forming a kind of Chinese swastika around the hearth; here too, however, the *tokonoma,* which harbours the scroll-painting, remains in its asymmetrical position. The stage of the *No*-plays is an asymmetrical structure. And a typical guest room in a modern dwelling house has four walls often differing from each other in their aspect and function. One wall, for example, will contain the *tokonoma* (ornamental recess); and this will face a sliding door that fills the entire breadth of the opposite "wall". A third wall consists of paper-windows opening to the garden, and the remaining wall is also a framework of paper-windows, sliding open to a corridor—or this fourth wall may be solid, with shelves concealed by sliding screens. An impression of great lightness and vividness is created by this arrangement; and the paralysing feeling of being contained in a box or cave, which visits sometimes the inhabitants of Western houses, is not allowed to arise.

CHINA: THE REALM OF SPACE

It is tempting to seek the reason for these Sino-Japanese polarities in the vast geographical differences of the regions that have generated or attracted, nurtured or moulded, the two great nations of Eastern Asia. Chinese civilisation seems one with China's wide plains. Its foundations were laid in the North, where the seasons appear to obey the laws of the agrarian calendar with the regularity of a celestial chronometer. Here the evenly balanced structure of the open spaces, obviously orientated to the cardinal points of the compass, has a visual force; and the alternating sequences of cold and heat, of periods assigned to weaving and agriculture, female and male work, in strict obedience of human ordinance to a cosmic order, partake of the nature of a constitution. The flow of time seems to have lost its corrosive as well as its creative power: here it is only spatial qualities that count.

Chinese dwellings are cut into the soil, moulded from it, or
10

joined to it in such a way that they appear to be parts of the earth's crust. Riding by night through the streets of a suburb of Peking one feels as if one were moving among tiny folds of ground as seen through a microscope. But as important as the telluric character of China is its openness to a merciless light. Every form appears naked, in all its grandeur and misery. There is no mystery —save in the silent bareness itself, in which every pore is revealed to the sky. Even Chinese ghost stories appear clear, diurnal, divested of horror and uncanniness, if compared with Western tales of this kind. The mere surface of things speaks in this cruelly indifferent light so loudly that the importance given in China to "face" becomes understandable; the social prestige of a man depends on the surface of certain situations as they become visible to the community through the medium of simple gestures.

The true greatness of China's classical form is embodied in her ancient bronze vessels, especially those of the late Shang and Chou periods, which I would hesitate to call "archaic"; for the Chou epoch would seem to correspond in our own cultural cycle to the ripest periods of the Middle Ages and the Renaissance. These vessels are answered in an antithetical fashion by the monochrome porcelain produced two thousand years later on Chinese soil. The essence of pure form—shapes enclosing, rising, engirdling, supporting, opening—can nowhere be learned better than from the Chou bronzes. The possibilities inherent in colour—pure green, blue, red, white—must be studied from Sung, Ming, and Ch'ing porcelain.

It is not man who dominates in this world, but Space itself, the all-embracing matrix of things and beings, becoming first manifest in absolute form, flowering finally into pure colour. Midway between these initial and those concluding expressions of the Chinese soul stand the spiritual visions of the T'ang poets and the Sung painters in which the outer world seems on the point of dissolving, into a sequence of subtle echoes, shadowy recollections of cloudlike images; these too, however, arose from the same soil that produced the most whole-hearted lovers of food, drink and embraces, and bear the mark of a spirit never dissociated from matter, an essence never to be separated from its aspect, a timeless presence.

JAPAN: THE REALM OF TIME

The soil of Japan, essentially a world of thousands of great, small, and minute islands, bays, and valleys, is as much partitioned off and irregular as the immense Chinese plains are open and uniform. The cross of the four cardinal points is everywhere overlaid by a graceful wilderness of hills, volcanic ranges, fields and forests. Symmetrical forms are rare, and so are moments of perfect calm and sure stability. Relentlessly this archipelago is rocked by seismic shocks, invaded by storms, showered and pelted with rain, encircled by clouds and mists. Japanese houses attach themselves only lightly to the soil; they survive earthquakes and hurricanes by not relying too much on their slender foundations; their virtue is in their swinging elasticity. There is a corresponding quality in the men and women who dwell in those houses. They are neither strongly built nor steadfast and unswerving, but after each disaster they are ready to begin a new phase of life without looking back; yet they carry into the future the whole past of their race, in minds incapable of forgetting. It is not space that rules this form of existence, but time, duration, spontaneous change, continuity of movement.

In a Japanese year there are only a few days on which land and sea unfold their panorama in clear contours under a changeless heaven. The scenery attains its greatest beauty when half-hidden in rain or mists, with mountains half-shrouded in clouds; it demands to be seen at the right moment, caught as it were by a swift light hand; thus it seems to have taught the art and value of veiling, covering, enclosing, hiding feelings and truths, presents and purposes. If Lao-tse's praise of the virtue of "hiddenness" and of "glare tempered" has become, through the aesthetics of Zen Buddhism, the guiding principle of what is most Japanese in Japanese art, its acclimatisation must have been favoured strongly by the most characteristic aspects of Japanese climate and topography. In contact with this new soil it seems to have gained a new meaning, or perhaps to have regained a very old one: for has there not been at the very root of Taoist wisdom an intuitive knowledge of the mysteries of life itself, an essence which cannot grow, and cannot renew itself, unless it is shielded by shadowy enclosures and surrounded by an atmosphere that does not allow each ray of light to pass through its protective filter? To preserve the germ of self-generating growth, and to shelter its slow instinct-bound development, no country is physically better equipped than the islands of Japan; to make an organism expand, exhibit and expose itself, none better than the plains of China.

NOTES

1 Lin Yutang, "The Aesthetics of Chinese Calligraphy", *T'ien Hsia Monthly*, Vol. 1, no. 5, 1935.
2 Sung Kuo-t'ing, "Lost tract of the marvels of calligraphy", translated by Sun Ta-yu, *T'ien Hsia Monthly*, Vol. 1, 1935, p. 19 *et seq.*
3 Minamoto Hoshu, *An Illustrated History of Japanese Art*, Kyoto, 1935, p. 209.
4 Oswald Siren, *Early Chinese Painting*, London, 1933, Vol. II, p. 93.
5 René Grousset, *The Civilization of the Far East: China*, London, 1931, p. 82 *et seq.*
6 Siren, *op. cit.*, Vol. II, p. 77.

9

The Samurai: Legend and Reality

TYPES OF NOBILITY

In every mature civilisation there seems to exist a normative image of the superior man, the *beau idéal* not of a single class or caste or profession or creed, but of the nation as a whole in its most characteristic and cherished traits and accomplishments. This image lives in a germinal form during those phases of a culture that may be called its spring and early summer; it gains consciousness and precision of outline during the autumnal stages and ends by becoming conventionalised and congealed. Of this type are the English gentleman, the Italian *cortegiano*, the French *gentilhomme*, the Greek *kalokagathos*, the Roman *vir honestus*, the Chinese *chün tzu* (the noble man of breeding). Their Japanese homologue is the *samurai*.

Each of these conceptions emerges, with a somewhat disturbing regularity, about one thousand years after a civilisation has risen from the level of tribal life. Its emergence marks the moment reached by a civilisation that has passed through the phases of archaic kingdom, hierocratic empire, and individualising urban life and is about to enter the stage of the secular territorial state. In this process the figures of the ruler, the warrior, the priest, the peasant, the artisan, have been differentiated from the stock of tribal communities with their scant and simple stratifications. To each of those types belongs a certain set of functions and privileges, of traditions and codes, within the broader sphere of social morality and institutional religion common to all.

The new ideal type appears at the moment when this monumental structure begins to disintegrate, so that religion and politics, art and literature, science and economy are gaining a state of autonomy denied to them in the age of Faith. Delivered into the grasp of conflicting forces, the unity of human life is in danger of proving too weak to withstand the demands of particular impulses and aspirations. The knight, the priest, the artisan, were characterised by their one function in the social organism; and this one service required the whole man and moulded all his activities and attitudes. In the new situation function has lost its integrating force together with its fixed place in the social universe. Its real character can best be gauged from the example of Germany, where no nation in the strict sense of the word exists, so that the people are actually represented by an aggregate of highly specialised individuals who find fulfilment through the performance of specific works, while lacking a normative central image, a significant gesture, a way of life sufficient to itself. The figures of the Prussian officer and the Prussian official may seem at first sight surrogates for such a central type; but they are defined through their functions, restricted to a class, and characterised by their incapacity to serve as a universal model even within a nation.

It is different with the gentleman, the *chün tzu*, the *vir honestus*, and other specimens of the *beau idéal* of mature civilisations. All these types arise from the ideas and attitudes of noblemen, but they acquire their normative identity not by the fact of noble birth or special service but by virtue of certain qualities of individual character and bearing. The knightly origin of these norms is not difficult to recognise, even in the case of China; but they owe their prestige as national ideal types to a peculiar blending of the old warrior virtues with the new spirit of "civility", to the indefinable but all-pervading presence of the qualities of gentleness, "sweetness and light", *sophrosyne, humanitas, jen* (reciprocity-mindedness), in which the ethical and religious teachings of an earlier age seem to have been distilled into a secular and more intimate set of standards. It is to the men (and women) embodying such standards that Schiller's words most aptly apply: "Common natures pay with what they *do;* noble natures with what they *are.*" Neither the performance of tasks nor the fulfilment of moral commands constitutes their goodness; this lies in their "being as they are".

Other men, recalling the memories of demi-gods or titans, may achieve wholeness in a wider compass by remoulding on a higher plane the primordial unity of life—poets and prophets, philosophers, saints and great rulers, who find in themselves the law of a new life and establish a new scale of values, infusing the souls of their first followers and, in broadening circles, the mind of their race, with a new conception of god and man. Of this mind they may be seen as the woof. The gentleman, the *chün tzu,* the *vir honestus,* the *cortegiano* form the warp. They are not creators or innovators, path-breakers and revolutionaries; through them the nation expresses what she thinks fit to serve as a normal standard of superior existence within the framework of society. Their role in this framework, their relation to the creative men of genius, their place in the metaphysical scheme operating within a community, may vary in the several societies that have given them birth. There is a world of difference between the all-round virtuosity of the *cortegiano* and the indifference of the gentleman, whose virtues and inclinations seem to be defined mostly in terms of avoidance and restraint. But these individual characteristics are best illumined by being seen against the background they have in common.

To do this for the Japanese samurai, the Japanese knight, and his code, usually called *bushido,* will serve, I hope, to clear away much of the polemical fog with which the subject has been for too long obscured. But it may be useful first to dwell for a moment on the strange way in which the West was made familiar with the existence of the samurai and his code.

THE DISCOVERY OF BUSHIDO

For almost half a century after Japan had been reopened to

foreign intercourse, she remained to the West a closed, recondite being, half veiled in legend, difficult of access, and inviting but a small number of lovers of exotic art, archaic custom, and mercantile profit. It was only after her decisive victory over Tsarist Russia in 1904–5 that she came to be regarded as a political force of the first order, able to influence the fate of Western nations and therefore inviting intellectual efforts to appraise her true character. Thus she justified the thought of those philosophers who derive the sense of reality, of objective existence, from feelings of resistance, of hardness experienced.

"We recognise", wrote a war-correspondent of that epoch, "almost grudgingly and in spite of ourselves, the existence of a moral force that appears able to govern and sway the whole conduct of a whole people, inspiring not a caste but a nation, from highest to lowest, to deeds that are worthy to rank among the most famous in history and legend. We want to know what this force is, whence it comes, and what it means; the sense of its existence makes us jealous, uncomfortable, almost annoyed."[1]

To this question an answer had been given by a Japanese scholar of great literary parts who possessed an intimate knowledge of the cultures of the East and of the West. This was Dr Inazo Nitobe, a samurai by birth, a Quaker by faith, and, later, one of the leading officials of the League of Nations.* In a number of books and essays, the first of which was published in 1899, he drew the attention of foreign readers to the existence of the Japanese warrior's moral code, *bushido*, in which Nitobe saw not only the "commanding moral force of his country", but also the "totality of the moral instincts of the Japanese race . . . in its elements coeval with our blood and therefore also with our religion of Shintoism."[2] The hyperbolic formula was so catching,

---

* Nitobe (1862–1933) was successively professor of Kyoto Imperial University, President of the First Higher School, professor of Tokyo Imperial University, and deputy-director of the general affairs bureau of the League of Nations secretariat (1920–27). [Ed.]

and Dr Nitobe's persuasive talent was so impressive, that many Western writers felt authorised to regard *bushido* as the common denominator of all they admired (or scorned) in Japanese life or politics.

In the years of the Anglo-Japanese alliance the admirable aspects of *bushido* seemed uppermost in Western minds. After the First World War, when Japan's claims to hegemony in the Far East began to delineate themselves rather clearly, the word *bushido* came to be uttered only with diffidence, and not seldom with a sneer. Dr Nitobe's account of the virtues of Samurai-Japan was discarded as romantic; yet his theory of *bushido* as the explanation of all Japan's national endowments and aspirations was retained, and henceforth everything Japan did and said was labelled *bushido*—including the Emperor cult and the expansionist foreign policy, Shinto and the "spirit of Japan" (*Yamato damashii*), and many things intensely disliked and courageously opposed by Dr Nitobe, an ardent pacifist and unflinching liberal, whose conflicts with the nationalist groups of army officers are well known. It is true that certain Japanese nationalist writers and societies made some use of the *bushido* theory—a fact that recalls the fate of Georges Sorel's theory of violence: which was, in his view, a weapon in the fight of the proletariat for emancipation; but it was applied eventually in Italy and Germany in the interests of the professed enemies of Bolshevism. Dr Nitobe was not responsible for the turgid statements of hyper-patriots. His only fault was to treat in a transport of unbridled enthusiasm a theme that demanded precise definition and historical sense.

ORIGINS OF THE WARRIOR CLASS

It is untrue, except in a narrow lexicographical sense, that the term *bushido* does not occur before the beginning of the twentieth century. Authoritative writings on the Way of the Warrior appeared two centuries earlier, in the Genroku period, some generations after the establishment of the Tokugawa Shogunate. Yamaga Soko was the head of an eminently influential military school, whose teachings are said to have kindled the spirit in which the Forty-Seven Ronin sacrificed their lives in avenging their lord's death, and whose spiritual descendant was Yoshida Shoin, the inspirer of those who led the Meiji Revolution. Yamaga Soko left a record of his lectures, a book called *Shido*—*shi* denoting the feudal retainer or gentleman, *do* meaning "the way", the norm, obligation, law (cognate with the Chinese *tao* and recalling the origins of the Greek *dike*). A smaller treatise by the same author is entitled *Bukyo-shogaku*—the Lesser (*sho*) School (*gaku*) of the Teachings (*kyo*) of the Samurai (*bu*). Evidently the idea of *bushido* remained unchanged, whether its verbal equivalent was *shido, bukyo,* or *budo* (as with Daidoji Yuzan, Yamaga Soko's pupil, author of the authoritative and sober *Budo Shoshinshu,* "A Primer of the Warrior's Way").*

Sir George Sansom observes that *bushido* is "a difficult subject leading into fruitless controversies".[3] I venture to think that it is not more difficult than any other major chapter in the history of moral and political thought; that most perplexities have arisen from careless use of terms and from emotional undertones or arguments; and that it is neither fruitless nor impossible to distinguish here between realities and words, historical facts and propagandist figments.

Unfortunately Professor Hall Chamberlain, the founder of Japanology, by an unguarded statement, so seldom seen in his careful writings, appears to have misled later commentators. In an essay entitled *The Invention of a New Religion,* first published

---

* Yamaga Soko (1622–1685) and Daidoji Yuzan (1639–1730) (also known as Daidoji Shigesuke) were both associated for a time with the *daimyo* family of Asano. It was the head of this house, Asano Naganori, who in 1701 was ordered to commit suicide by the Shogunate for attacking a high official, Kira Yoshinaka, in the palace at Yedo. (The latter had grossly provoked and insulted Asano.) It was the revenge carried out by certain of Asano's retainers that became immortalised in print and on the Kabuki stage as the tale of the Forty-Seven Ronin. The moral of that tale is not so much the revenge, planned and executed at the price of much personal sacrifice, as the fact that the forty-seven retainers surrendered themselves to justice as soon as they had killed Kira Yoshinaka. This respect for the law, it has been claimed, was induced by the teachings of Yamaga and Daidoji, both of whom had been attached to the Asano household. [Ed.]

in 1912 and, from 1927, appearing as an Appendix in *Things Japanese* (in the last edition not prepared by himself) he affirms:

"Bushido, as an institution or a code of rules, has never existed. The accounts given of it have been fabricated out of whole cloth, chiefly for foreign consumption. . . . The very word appears in no dictionary, native or foreign, before the year 1900. . . . Neither Kaempfer, Siebold, Satow, nor Rein—all men knowing their Japan by heart—ever once alludes to it in their voluminous writings. The cause of their silence is not far to seek. Bushido was unknown until a decade or so ago."[4]

This statement, however, proves too little and too much. If *bushido* (the Way of the Warrior) is a term and thing unknown before 1900 it follows that it cannot have been a myth invented or used in order to support the Meiji monarchy, which at that late date needed no such artificial underpinning. As for Dr Nitobe —his liberal convictions and affiliations are so well known that the emergence of the title and theory of *bushido* under his name cannot be construed as a machination of governmental or hyper-patriotic origin. It can be shown, moreover, that for good reasons the patriotic literature of the Meiji period, and well beyond that period, preferred to appeal to other ethical doctrines rather than to the Way of the Warrior, the moral heritage of the unruly *samurai*. It was only later that references to the samurai virtues appeared in the programmes of nationalist associations with greater, although (except in propaganda for foreign consumption) not conspicuous, frequency—a paradoxical but not uncommon reflex of foreign styles of thinking observable in the ideas of Japanese nationalists.

Japanese scholars innocent of propagandist leanings, such as Professor Masaharu Anesaki, have traced the origin of such teachings to the Kamakura period and the subsequent "times of trouble" under the Hojo regents and Ashikaga shoguns; when a new class of warriors rose to power and, in a long laborious process, made the military fief the administrative and economic foundation of a unified feudal government, with its seat first at Kamakura and later in Muromachi, Kyoto. This new class was in a typically Japanese fashion at the same time archaic and revolutionary, loyalist and anarchic. It was led by great families, claiming Imperial descent, that had built up for themselves an imposing house-power far from the capital in semi-autonomous country districts, based on a kind of manorial economy.

The new class of warriors originated when the conscription system of the bureaucratic monarchy introduced from China fell into decay, and when the rise of the *sho-en* (immunities of quasi-manorial character) led to a demand for courageous and determined men willing to protect manorial estates in times of wide-spread unrest and uncertain allegiances. The warriors were recruited from the peasant class, from families of former provincial notables, and from the dissatisfied and adventurous residuum existing in the crevices of every society.

To weld these heterogeneous elements together under the guidance of the local branches of the great metropolitan houses was no mean achievement; and it is much to the credit of the Kamakura rulers that a spiritual foundation for the solution of the problem was sought in the new school of Zen meditation introduced into Japanese Buddhism from China, with its ideals of serenity and simplicity, calm resignation, rock-like determination undismayed by death, and mystic realisation of the unity of all beings.

The first written testimonies of the new spirit were the *yuikai* ("teachings left", or spiritual legacies) and *kakun* (family laws). These moral instructions, addressed by clan heads to their descendants, were held in reverent regard by their families and their retainers. Their faith was Buddhist: it was impregnated by the belief in the interdependence of all cosmic life, thought and action; but they continued to invoke the help and protection of Shinto deities and ancestral spirits. Of the *yuikai* and *kakun* Professor Anesaki observes that in these documents "the practice of loyalty to the sovereign and fidelity to family traditions" was strongly underlined, and "the virtues of charity, justice, honesty, modesty, valour were also included". Anesaki goes on:

"Advice was given to the heirs of military leaders as to administration of feudal territories, treatment of soldiers, care of provisions, and as to codes of honour in peace and war. In short, religious beliefs and worldly wisdom, spiritual training, military discipline, moral ideals and practical counsels were fused into the one principle of the warrior's honour. The principle and practice of *bushido*, the Way of the Warrior, found here definite formulation, and these teachings were destined to sway the ruling classes throughout coming centuries. Some of these documents exercised an influence beyond the limits of the clans and families and became in some respects a national heritage."[5]

The house-laws of military clans, including those of the ruling family of the Tokugawa clan, are the linear descendants of these early spiritual legacies. To withhold from them the name of code or institution is only possible if the use of these terms is unduly restricted to rigid systems resembling the *Deuteronomium*, the *Institutions* of Justinian, or the *Code Napoléon*. The contents of the Samurai-laws retained a certain fluidity and plasticity; this kept them alive and able to survive in periods of violent change and revolutionary ferment. To deny that they had a decisive influence on the formation of the Japanese character and of Japanese thought and society is to allow oneself to be blinded by one's own scepticism. Neither Hall Chamberlain nor Sansom, although ready to discount much that is contained in hyperbolical eulogies, has carried his disbelief in any superior congenital moral quality of the Japanese so far as to declare the ethics of the samurai to be mere legend, artificially constructed in the Meiji period for political purposes. It was a pattern of ideas and ideals clothed with the authority first of the clan head or the ruler, later of the military scholar and patriotic leader. Instead of denouncing it as a fiction, one ought to dwell on the abyss that separates the genuine ethics of the samurai from recent ideologies patterned upon the pseudomyths of contemporary European totalitarianism.

THE RELIGIOUS BACKGROUND

Far from being a creed demanding the expansion of the Japanese Empire, the rule of the sword, and the subjugation of foreign people by the descendants and retainers of the Children of the Sun, the ethics of the samurai belonged essentially to a *static* world moulded by Buddhist feeling and Confucian thought. The Christian knight sought "adventure" in order to prove his prowess; to fight against uncouth villains, giants, and devilish monsters, in defence of women and the poor; to serve the Church and to further the triumph of Christianity. A straight line leads from the Paladins of Charlemagne and the Knights of Arthur's Round Table to the Crusades and to the Conquistadores. They are all attracted by unconquered spaces and the lure of the *mission* with all its possibilities of adventure. The samurai does not experience such urges; which lead the knight on and on into the vast darkness of the unknown, riding like the *miles Christianus* of Dürer's engraving through perilous forests infested by Death and the Devil.

Zen meditation has taught the true samurai the way inward. His is a will to enter the sphere where there is no fear of dying nor hope of after-life, because the borderline between life and death has been experienced as illusory. This inward sphere does not demand meritorious deeds, because good and evil have lost their childlike simplicity. To be moved by transports of enthusiasm and fighting ardour, carried as it were on the surge of a great wave crashing against the cliffs of fate, is not his ambition: rather it is to become like a rock on which the waves of life rush in vain. He who attains enlightenment has left far behind him churches, holy books, sacred images, and theological dogma. He has regained that pristine state in which the soul becomes one with the Absolute, and in which a new power of determination springs up from depths that are unfathomable.

Buddhist ethics appear, at least to Western eyes, negative and preparatory rather than normative and creative. In Zen the main concerns are to be freed from impediments of salvation, to be subject no longer to "hunger" in all its various forms, to eliminate the distinction between I and You, Good and Evil, Man and the Whole, Life and Death—and not to shape this life of ours according to some divine image. The ethics of the samurai centre on the teachings of how to die, how to be undismayed, unmoved, unshakeable, free from all-too-human interests and entanglements. From this height of an amoral (not necessarily immoral) mysticism a steep short path leads to the regions of nihilism and quietism. But it would not be quite fair to make Zen meditation responsible for what it sometimes became in dull and in dissolute souls. Similar dangers mark the way of every religion and first attract the attention of critics alien to that creed.

I am not trying to maintain that the average samurai did partake of ultimate enlightenment. But his thought was moving in a spiritual magnetic field, the pole of which was not action in the outer world, but annihilation of externals, readiness for sacrifice and for complete self-abnegation. The treatises on *bushido* written in the first half of the Tokugawa era contain, it is true, many exhortations not to neglect training in arms and not to think war a remote possibility, and with good reason; for this was a period in which the warrior had become a kind of official, exposed to the lures of a luxuriant growth of urban pleasures in an age of systematic seclusion, thorough pacification and political stagnation.

Here too, however, the dominant note remained the insistence on a mental discipline able to subdue the desire for personal enjoyment and gain, laziness and licence, and to keep awake the readiness for service. The style of every activity the samurai might indulge in, the performance of the tea ceremony, the singing of *utai*, the practice of archery as well as of the ceremonial for committing suicide—all bear the imprint of such discipline; the monkish colour of garments echo its spirit. To achieve complete mastery of one's natural inclinations, to attain unruffled serenity in utter adversity, not to exult in triumph nor to yield to sorrow, are the main objects of this code of behaviour. The No-play preserves the ascetic style of this life more faithfully than any treatise or anecdote. It shows that we are confronted here not with doctrinaire demands and vain transports, but with a form of life that has been lived, certainly in various degrees of purity and vigour, but a life unquestionably real, of great dignity and austere beauty.

IDEALS AND REALITIES

Form everywhere easily degenerates into mere formalism, courage into brawling, loyalty into servility, calmness into insensitivity. Later writers, in extolling the samurai spirit, have often dwelt on the virtues of martial bravery and one-sided loyalty as if they had been the pillars of samurai ethics. Commonplace courage, however, cannot be termed the inspiring force of *bushido*. The warriors who, from the end of the Heian age, flocked to the banners of the new feudal leaders of Japan needed no exhortation to physical bravery; they delighted in fighting and were not much afraid of losing their poor lives. What the heads of clans on their death-beds, the chiefs of feudal governments in their codes and injunctions, felt urged to infuse into the sturdy and crude minds of their retainers was a spiritual conception of their duties, a discipline moulding the whole life of the warrior, an image of the Right Life that if sincerely lived could justify the warrior's claim to dominion over the other classes. The samurai was not to be a man of more rights, but of more duties.

These duties were not one-sided. In a typical oath and pledge exchanged by lord and retainer in southern Kyushu late in the fifteenth century, the retainer swears that he will serve the lord "with single devotion and without a second thought", while the lord, acknowledging the promise of loyalty, replies: "I will regard your important affairs as my own, and we will mutually rely and be relied upon; if despite this understanding a calumny or an evil report should arise, we would mutually explain ourselves, with complete frankness."[6] The lord's pledge is put under the sanction of the most dreaded deities of mediaeval Japan, including the sun-goddess of Ise, Hachiman (the war-god), and the deities of Kumano and Suwa. An obligation protected by such deities cannot at that period be considered as a mere formality.

As in every relation between men unequal in power, wealth and rank, it is reasonable to expect that in practice the strict balance between the rights of the lord and of the retainer would not always have remained untilted. In the East, where patriarchal structures dominated all social and political thought, it was almost unavoidable that the retainer's duties should be assimilated by those of filial piety; this occurred in classical Chinese thought and survived in the *bushido* teachings of such Japanese as Yamaga Soko and Yuzan; the more the lord assumed the authority of a father the more it tended to become absolute, for according to Oriental notions the son had no rights against his sire. But in Japan, as in China and in the European Middle Ages, the retainer had not only the right but also the duty to remonstrate whenever he deemed the lord's action unjust or inappropriate. A samurai who blindly fulfilled the will of his lord against the voice of his own conscience was called a *neishin* (cringeling, fawning parasite) or *choshin* ("a favourite who steals his master's affections by means of servile compliance"—Nitobe[7]). If all efforts at persuasion failed, the retainer's protest had to take the form of suicide (*seppuku*).

Instances of disloyalty, and of samurai changing sides, during the centuries of internal troubles and civil wars are frequently reported in the Japanese chronicles; but only a biased mind could undertake to estimate the proportion these cases bore to normal loyal behaviour. Questions of honour are singularly ill-suited for statistical treatment. We have no means of knowing whether the majority of the samurai—or, for that matter, any class in any country—did or did not remain below the standard set by codes and treatises. The very existence of literary admonitions shows that the virtues the samurai was asked to cultivate were not expected to spring up spontaneously. Yuzan, the greatest authority on Tokugawa *bushido*, says clearly that many sumarai had only inferior grades of qualities. To take *bushido* as a natural quality inherent in the Japanese race is a mistake reserved for

11

later writers seduced by easy biologisms. Until the end of the nineteenth century there was no attempt to deny that, for Japanese too, *bushido* was difficult to achieve. But it was not thought impossible. In fact, it is a gratuitous assumption to state that the higher *bushido* teachings remained mainly on paper, without becoming a living force in the life of real men, stronger and weaker men alike.

At all times, and with all groups, the demands of higher systems of ethics have been fulfilled only by a moral élite in a position to impose their standards on populations unable to live up to them, yet unable at the same time to deny the righteousness of such standards. There was, however, a better chance of a samurai fulfilling the norms of *bushido* than a Christian living according to the teachings of the Sermon on the Mount, with its paradoxical if not hyperbolical demands. To be generous, dutiful, circumspect, obeying father and authorities, frugal, sober, diligent, and composed in the face of death or misery: all this is not according to everybody's nature; but it imposes less strain on the psychic structure of natural man than the demand to love one's enemies and to tender the right cheek after the left cheek has been struck.

It was the historic mission of the Tokugawa age to inject the spirit of the samurai into ever-widening circles of Japanese society, in attenuated vigour and purity, but not necessarily in a debased form. It was a movement resulting in one of the most complete democratisations of an aristocratic set of ideals of which history has left us a trace. Even the attitudes of the housewife and the student, the shop apprentice and the courtesan, mirrored, in suitable diminution, the attitude of the feudal retainer to his lord

The tremendous wave of enthusiasm aroused in the quarters of the ordinary town-dweller by the heroic vendetta of the Forty-Seven Ronin demonstrates that the spirit of the samurai has ceased to be a class-morality at the beginning of the eighteenth century. The merchant and artisan townsman recognised the values for which the samurai lived and died to be at the centre of national ethics: and this popular wave of emotional adherence must have been no less effective than the revival of the Ancient Learning and of primeval Shinto in preparing the way for the final welding together, five generations later, of all classes into the modern nation. While the West bade farewell to the spirit of the feudal age in the historical plays of Shakespeare and Cervantes' *Don Quixote*, in Japan this spirit expanded, duly diluted, into the minds of the rice dealers and luggage-carriers of the greatest metropolis of those times, Yedo, later Tokyo: and the typical "Yedokko", the common man of its streets and shops, was proud to live his life in a manner that would have pleased Don Quixote rather than Sancho Panza.

There is, of necessity, a danger inseparable from all such vulgarisations of high-strung moral ideas. The citizen of the great towns, his wife and his courtesan-lovers, were attracted to *bushido* mainly by the forces of sentiment, and often by a desire for what was strange, colourful, and exciting: to such demands one answer was the drama of the Tokugawa era, the *kabuki*, an inexhaustible source of strong emotion, unheard-of action, intense colour, and expression carried to the limit of the grotesque. All this was alien to the true samurai spirit, whose canon can be gauged from the style of the *No*-play, austere, calm, subdued, and chaste. Thus it occurred that the life of the samurai was presented to the commoner in its extreme cases, verging on crime and madness, and placing strains on the sensibility and humanity of the theatre-goers that made, and continue to make, the parterre often swim in tears and the gallery explode in raucous cries of ecstatic acclamation.

The foreigner, finding access to the *No* difficult for both internal and external reasons, was easily fascinated by the *Kabuki-za* and by the tales written for Western readers in the early days, which were both readable and crudely illustrated; his impressions must have been reinforced by the hyper-dramatic actor-woodcuts of the *ukiyoe* school of popular artists. He was thus misled into taking these variations on samurai themes for the essence of *bushido*. Hence came the apparently ineradicable Western tendency to think of the samurai as a grotesquely gesticulating half-savage habitually murdering his own children for the benefit of his Lord, sending his wife to a brothel in order to buy a good steed, and finally committing suicide in skilfully prolonged agonies. These are famous themes of Japanese literature, but it would be as wrong to regard them as typical of the Way of the Warrior as to consider eating from a leper's bowl or living on the top of a column to be characteristic of ordinary Christian life. All these enter the class of "flagrant cases", not to be explained away, but to be relegated to the border region to which they belong.

The great Tokugawa treatises on *bushido*, by Yamaga Soko and Yuzan, do not even mention such extremes. Their tone is moderate, their teaching sensible; they never exaggerate the demands of a single virtue, and their scale of values bears no trace of a soldier caste bent upon self-glorification. Their teaching breathes an atmosphere jejune and colourless and is inspired either by the late Confucianist Sung philosophy of Chu-hsi (first introduced by Zen monks and some centuries later adopted as State orthodoxy), or by more interpid thinkers eager to discard the Sun commentators and their static ethics of conformity, so convenient to authoritarian rule. These bolder spirits groped their way back to the pure springs of early Confucianism. Compared with the Zen warriors of earlier ages there is certainly a loss of spiritual tension, but until the end the attainment of spiritual freedom remains the central virtue.

To determine to what extent the behaviour of modern Japanese is still shaped by the teachings of *bushido* is an undertaking as difficult as to assess the degree to which Christian ethics still mould the actions and bearing of contemporary Europeans. The Meiji Restoration was the work of the samurai, mainly of lower rank, with strong economic grievances and fierce patriotic passions, but it led to the abolition of the samurai class by the new State. The loss of powerful privileges; the continuation and, as often as not, the aggravation of their financial difficulties, above all for those samurai who did not find a suitable place in the new social framework as officers, officials or entrepreneurs, policemen or farmers; the unfulfilled hopes of glorious military enterprises discarded by the prudent Meiji Emperor and his chief adviser: all this led to much discontent among the former samurai, who sought redress by rebellious undertakings, unceasing agitation and occasional assassinations. To one familiar with these well-known facts it must appear quite unlikely that the authorities could have made any attempt to establish *bushido*—the spirit of the most troublesome class in the land—as the foundation of the new State ethics.

What happened in the Meiji era was not that *bushido* was made the basis of State ethics, but that loyalty was redefined and given a new content and orientation. For at least five hundred years *bushido* itself had been, in terms of practical politics, dissociated from service to the Imperial House. The loyalty of the samurai was mainly due to his feudal lord, the *daimyo*; and some of the most celebrated deeds of the samurai had been performed in assisting their *daimyo* against Imperial armies. But the "loyal men" who died in the Ueno battle and at Wakamatsu were, in the eyes of the Emperor, rebels against Imperial Rule. The idea that true loyalty was due to the Emperor only became the official guiding principle of political conduct during the Meiji era. No *bushido* myth was invented; but feelings and attitudes, based on a mythical tradition that had remained for seven centuries overshadowed by the rule of the samurai class, were re-established in order to annihilate the wrong work and confused loyalties of the feudal age—a process recalling the rehabilitation of Roman myths and cults by the Emperor Augustus.

If the past state and future possibilities of Japan are to be gauged correctly, it is of paramount importance to distinguish these processes from the political and propagandist fictions produced at the beginning of the twentieth century. The Emperor-myth and the samurai tradition are genuine; but in recent decades they have been exploited as tools of nationalist and imperialist propaganda and thereby discredited. Yet it would be not only against historical truth, but also detrimental to sound political judgement, to mistake them for phenomena of the same order of flimsiness as such purposive paper-myths as "The White Man's Burden", "The General Strike", or "The Nordic Race".

Survival of the samurai tradition is far from being a literary phenomenon. When the samurai class as such was abolished, its ideals remained in force, unquestioned. Even now it is often possible to distinguish by their bearing and action Japanese of samurai stock from those of commoner's origin (*heimin*). It was only during the China Incident* that the distinction between samurai and *heimin* was removed from a man's registration papers.

The pre-war curriculum of the State schools, at least until not long before the Second World War, was not responsible for any artificial stimulation of martial interests. The school system of the Meiji era was liberal in outlook, and the examples illustrating ethical teaching were drawn from a wide range of facts in which the samurai tradition occupied no greater space than any country would devote to the meritorious deeds of her own past. It would be a serious mistake to believe that it was governmental propaganda that made the modern Japanese ready to fling their lives away and suffer what appears intolerable.

Not all the disregard for life and happiness, verging on a passionate desire to sacrifice oneself for the good of the national whole, can be ascribed to the samurai tradition. There lives in the Japanese both the mind of the tribe, compelling the individual to surrender before the needs of the human beehive, and the soul of the mystic, finding supreme fulfilment in abandoning a self conceived to be one with the Soul of the Universe, or Buddha. Between these two extremes, limiting cases of human morals, the Way of the Samurai, like every ethic of a chivalrous type, holds an intermediate position, drawing strength from both sources.

To the Japanese the true character of the samurai is expressed

---

* The China Incident refers to the undeclared war between Japan and China that erupted in the summer of 1937. In Higher Schools up to that period the nominal rolls of students still had a column listing the social origins of the pupils at the school. [Ed.]

in the cherry-blossoms; which suddenly open under the morning sun and as suddenly fall to the ground when shaken by the winds of spring. If the foreign reader experiences a certain difficulty in reconciling this image with what he has seen of, and read about, the callous insensitivity and unbridled violence of Japanese warriors, let him follow the course of history upstream, and he can find in the story of Taira Atsumori an indication of what the symbol meant before it became a conventional formula. When after the fatal defeat at Ichi-no-tani by the hands of Yoritomo the Taira clan sailed from the main island, Atsumori, a nephew of the great Kiyomori, was the last to leave the shore. Challenged by one of the strongest of the enemy warriors, he turned his horse back, fought against the greatest odds and was killed. When his adversary looked beneath the helmet of the slain, he discovered the smiling face of a boy of fifteen, and in the folds of his armour a piece of precious brocade containing a famous flute made out of Chinese bamboo. On the eve of the fight, the Taira had held a festival in the shadow of impending disaster, with music filling the last hours before defeat and death overcame them.[8]

The world is not rich enough in dreams of knighthood to make light of such images of heroic serenity and refined ardour, virile intrepidity and spiritual aloofness. The fighting instincts and the aesthetic sense of the Japanese race have here been tempered by Indian mystical thought and Chinese cosmic ceremonial. It is in this spirit penetrating every detail of life in peace and war, poetry and archery, ritual and leisure that we may find the true measure of the Japanese mind. For it is not to be discovered in an abstract idea, or system, or work of art, or institution. The image and the spirit do not attain the beauty of the Greek Miracle or the transcendent Grace descending on the Christian's Passion. But they have given an example of daring blended with delicacy, firmness allied to lightness, transport to taste; an exquisite achievement the memory of which should not be allowed to be tainted by the all too common misuses to which the figure of the samurai has often been subjected in an epoch of universal disorder and growing confusion.

If a nation has strayed far from the centre of her true greatness, the task is not to make her forget her past, but to remind her of the true meaning of her deepest inspirations and her highest dreams. Thus, after a general and total expiation, the ravaged earth may be prepared for a new beginning; which an Asian nation may conceive as a return to the Way of which Lao-tse has spoken:

> *"In it all sharpness is blunted*
> *All tangles untied*
> *All glare tempered*
> *All dust smoothed."*[9]

NOTES

1 William Stead, *Great Japan*, London, no date, p. 38.
2 Nitobe's essay in W. Stead, *Japan by the Japanese*, London, 1904, pp. 266, 279.
3 G. B. Sansom, *Japan, A Short Cultural History*, New York, 1943, p. 495.
4 B. Hall Chamberlain, *Things Japanese*, London, 1927, p. 564.
5 M. Anesaki, *A History of Japanese Religion*, London, 1930, p. 222.
6 K. Asakawa, *Documents of Iriki*, New Haven, 1929, pp. 295–6.
7 I. Nitobe, *Bushido*, London, 1907, p. 92.
8 Noel Peri, *Cinq No; drames lyriques japonais*, Paris, 1921, pp. 216–19.
9 Arthur Waley, *The Way and its Power*, London, 1934, p. 146.
"Dust is the Taoist symbol for the noise and fuss of everyday life." *(ibid.)* It is this passage, in a slightly different interpretation ("tempered glare, united to the dust"), which has in Japan been cherished by the Buddhists of the Tendai sect and by the writers of the No-plays. K.S.)

Index

Index